RELATIONSHIP BOOTCAMP

Hard-Core Training for Life, Love & the Pursuit of Intimacy

By

ROY BIANCALANA

Foreword by Jim Dethmer

This book is published by Roy A. Biancalana

Many self-help books contain disclaimers designed to protect the author from being sued if (or when?) the reader discovers the book's wisdom doesn't work. No such disclaimer occurs here. If you follow the path outlined in this book, you *will* get "in shape" and be fully prepared to experience an amazing, sustainable, intimate relationship.

ISBN: 978-1-7333014-0-4

Cover design and graphics by Mike Brucher

ARE YOU IN RELATIONSHIP "SHAPE"?

Introducing...

The Relationship Fitness Self-Assessment Test

Before you read this book, take five minutes and answer thirty true/false questions to discover your relationship fitness level.

Knowing your current relationship "condition" will make this book that much more meaningful to you.

Find out if you are relationally *ripped, skinny fat, overweight, unhealthy* or *dangerously out of shape.*

Get your assessment now at:

https://coachingwithroy.com/the-relationship-fitness-self-test/

OTHER RESOURCES FROM ROY BIANCALANA

ONLINE RELATIONSHIP BOOTCAMPS

These are 7-week group-coaching programs that focus intensely on the seven inner relationships discussed in this book. Limited to 10 people and done via Zoom video conferencing, they are fun, life-changing—and inexpensive! If you want to more fully explore any of the topics discussed in this book, this is a great option. Visit www.coachingwithroy.com for more information.

INDIVIDUAL COACHING

If you are interested in attracting a healthy, sustainable, intimate relationship, then working directly with Roy is your best option. He offers a free (no pressure) consultation to see if his training (coaching) program is a good fit for you. For more information, email him at coachingwithroy@gmail.com.

BOOKS

Roy has written two other books, both of which are #1 best-sellers:
- A Drink with Legs: *From Being "Hooked" to Being Happy—A Spiritual Path to Relationship Bliss*
- Attracting Lasting Love: *Breaking Free of the 7 Barriers that Keep You Single*

ECOURSES

For those who prefer watching video to reading books, Roy has created a number of different professionally-done, video-based eCourses that address the most relevant issues in a single person's life. They can all be found at www.coachingwithroy.com. Two of the most popular are:
- The Radiant Woman: *Being the Woman that Evokes a Man's Full Devotion*
- The Superior Man: *Being the Man Every Woman Wants and the World Desperately Needs*

COACH-TRAINING

Roy offers a one-year *Coach-Training & Certification Program* for those who want to become coaches, making an impact on people's lives and a great income doing it. For information, click <u>HERE</u> or email Roy at <u>coachingwithroy@gmail.com</u>.

DEDICATION

To my "personal trainers" …

Jim Dethmer, Michael Singer, Diana Chapman,
David Deida & Eckhart Tolle

―――――――――――――――

"An unexamined life is not worth living."

~ Socrates

―――――――――――――――

TABLE OF CONTENTS

FOREWORD

by

Jim Dethmer

Co-author of *The 15 Commitments of Conscious Leadership*

I've known Roy Biancalana for almost thirty years. During that time, he's been interested in three things: golf, consciousness and relationships. He is passionate about all three. But he is more than passionate. He is persistent and practiced. What I mean by this is that he is not casual or laissez-faire.

There are millions of golfers in the world and a miniscule number of them become professional golfers. Roy did. It takes more than passion. Persistence and practice are required. Every being on the planet is conscious but few make consciousness a lifetime quest. Roy has. And billions of people have relationships, but a very small number have exquisite ones. Those who do are devoted to a set of principles and they practice, day in and day out. They are persistent.

It is these last two passions, consciousness and relationships, that I assume have brought you to this book. In my experience, you have come to a good place. Roy knows relationships. First and foremost, he's a devoted practitioner and life-long learner in his own intimate relationships. He "eats his own cooking," you could say. And secondly, because he's coached countless others on how to create quality partnerships, you can trust his process.

This is not to say that his process is easy. As Roy says over and over, it's difficult. Choosing to have Roy as your relationship trainer means serious work, straight talk and lasting results. But you have to get your metaphorical relational butt in the gym and stay there. Roy will give you the principles and he'll show you all the key questions, but it's your responsibility to sit, be still, reflect with curiosity, own your stuff and commit with full intention. If you do this, you'll succeed.

Now, as to that last statement, succeed at what? This is a *sleight of hand* on Roy's part, though he is honest about it from the start. What you'll succeed at is waking up, becoming aware, learning how to source life and love from the inside, and finally, how to be a partner who is available for, and capable of, great relationships. I say, "sleight of hand," because I imagine you picked up this book to help you find a great partner, a lover, an intimate other—and in the end, you might get that. But what I KNOW you'll get is a relationship with yourself and with LIFE and LOVE that will so fill you, liberate you, and invigorate you, that you'll be happy to have a great relationship—and you'll no longer *need* one.

One of the things I appreciate about Roy is that he takes on commonly held beliefs and deconstructs and debunks them. This is risky business and it's risky for you to read these parts of the book—especially if the commonly held beliefs are yours. But this is what a great coach does. They tell you what you're doing and believing that won't work and they give you new ideas and practices that will.

One such belief that Roy takes on is the Law of Attraction. For many years, this belief has been at the center of manifestation philosophy and it has been taught and espoused by wonderful and powerful teachers. It has been taught because it works, and as Roy points out, that is exactly the problem. Unless we do the deep work to unwind our unconscious beliefs and commitments, we will attract something we won't want once we get it. Wow. He invites us to stop making lists of the characteristics we desire in an ideal partner because, in essence, we'll make the wrong list.

Roy takes you to the taproot of desire, the core of the issue, and helps you excavate the underlying issues that keep you feeling separate and alone.

Once this is seen and the deep work is done, you're truly available for a relationship and you won't need a list.

The fourth "workout" in the book, *Strengthening Your Relationship to the Past,* is probably the most comprehensive description of the issues and practices for resolving one's past that I have ever read. Regardless of whether you're looking to create a lasting, conscious relationship or just be a free, peaceful, creative, loving person, this workout is a must for all of us.

I've spent the last 40 years committed to becoming more awake and conscious and supporting thousands of others to do the same. I've co-authored best-selling books and talked to tens of thousands of people about how to have great relationships. What you have in this book is a comprehensive training manual written by an expert on how to create the kind of relationships you most deeply want and how to become the person you hunger to be.

Enjoy!
Jim Dethmer

A NOTE FROM THE AUTHOR

Dear Reader,

The famous Swiss psychiatrist, Carl Jung, once said, "There is no birth of consciousness without pain." Well, I have certainly found that to be true in my life. To whatever degree that I am a conscious, self-aware being, it is mostly because of the pain I've experienced in my intimate relationships. My painful love life has been the portal to profound personal growth, and for that I am grateful, because it drove me to look for answers—about myself, about relationships and about life itself—and the result is this book.

Since 2003, when my first marriage ended in divorce, I've been on a mission to understand why relationships are so often difficult and disappointing. That quest not only caused me to deeply introspect, but it led me to seek out numerous spiritual gurus, relationship experts and world-famous psychologists. I sat at their feet, I studied their teachings, and I poured over their research. And what I learned not only changed my life, but it has enabled me to create a loving, committed and wildly fulfilling relationship with my wife.

What follows, then, is everything I've learned on my incredible journey to understand "life, love and the pursuit of intimacy." It is my hope and desire that it changes your life as much as it has mine.

Now, as you can tell by the book's title, I'm using a fitness metaphor to communicate its message. However, you do not have to be a *physical* fitness fanatic to understand or benefit from this book. In fact, you can be a total "couch potato" and this book will still change your life. The fitness metaphor is merely an attempt to make the book interesting and fun to read.

Having said that—and continuing with the fitness metaphor—by reading this book you are asking me to be your "personal trainer" and I am truly honored to serve you in that way. But don't be fooled by the playful metaphor. This book is ***hard-core*** relationship training. It's written for those who are very serious about their growth and getting in the best relationship "shape" of their lives.

And here's my promise: If you do the seven "workouts" described in this book, although you're going to be "sore" in places you didn't even know existed, I guarantee that every drop of "sweat" will have been worth it, because in the end, you will be relationally "fit," completely prepared to experience a healthy, sustainable, intimate relationship, and I know that's what you most deeply want.

Now, before we begin, let me tell you a little bit about the structure of the book. The Prologue and the Epilogue function much like the *before* and *after* photos in a weight loss commercial.

The Prologue gives you a *before bootcamp* picture of "Harry" and "Sally," two typical single people who recently met online and are now about to physically meet for the first time. However, as you'll see, they are both relationally "out of shape."

Harry is lonely, insecure and dealing with confidence issues, and because Sally has been deeply hurt and betrayed by a former partner, she has trust issues. But don't get hung up on their genders. Women can have confidence issues and men can have trust issues. Just see if you can relate to any of their feelings, fears and frustrations.

The Epilogue, conversely, gives you an *after bootcamp* picture of the same people. Again, they are meeting for the first time, but because they've previously done the "workouts" in this book, they're "in shape" and ready to connect in a conscious and sustainable way. So, the Epilogue shows you what's possible if you don't just read this book but *live it.*

Roy Biancalana
St. Charles, Illinois
October 2019

PROLOGUE

When Harry Met Sally

Even though this was only their first official date, Harry was already thinking Sally could be "the one." He was so excited to meet her. In fact, he had been thinking about this moment ever since they met online about a week ago. Not only were her pictures gorgeous, but they had a couple of great phone conversations too. Harry knew it was crazy to get so far ahead of himself, but Sally truly seemed different from all the other women he had met. And he had met quite a few since his fiancée broke up with him three months ago.

Harry would never admit it, but that break-up had done a number on his confidence. He wasn't sure who he was anymore, and he certainly had no idea what women wanted—other than it seemed they didn't want him. And the loneliness he was feeling was profound, too. Without someone in his life, he felt lost and untethered. Being single sucked, and he was hoping Sally would change that.

After his break-up, his friends told him to take some time and be on his own. They thought he needed to grieve and to learn from what he'd been through. Blah, blah, blah. No way. Harry felt that the best way to deal with the pain and loneliness was to "get back on the horse." And yet he didn't know if his heart could handle another rejection. What was he going to do if Sally didn't like him? Harry felt trapped. On the one hand, he desperately wanted her to be "the one," but on the other, he was terrified that she wouldn't feel the same way. *What is wrong with me?* he thought.

Well, if you asked his ex, she would say Harry was needy and insecure. She told him as much when they had their last big fight, the one that ended with her pulling the ring off her finger. She said that no matter how much attention or affection she gave him, it was never enough. She said she was exhausted from feeling the constant pressure to make him feel special, and that no matter how hard she tried, he still seemed disappointed with her. She just couldn't take it anymore.

Well, that rocked Harry's world. Yes, he could be a little "relationally intense"—probably something to do with his mom working all the time when he was little and never being around—but he thought women liked that! Well, evidently not. What was he going to do? Who was he supposed to be in order to get a woman to love him? *What do women want?*

As he walked into the restaurant to meet Sally, even though he was very confused, one thing was crystal clear: he couldn't let on how much he was already into her. She might think he was needy and insecure—just like his ex did—and she'd bolt. So, he decided on a new strategy. He was going to be cool and confident, maybe even a bit aloof. That's why he was 15-minutes late to their date. He did it on purpose because he didn't want to appear desperate.

Walking in, he saw her sitting at the bar. *Damn, she's beautiful,* he thought, but he immediately caught himself. *Play it cool, you idiot. Play it cool.* "Sally? Harry. Nice to meet you. Sorry I'm late. Traffic. Can I buy you a drink?"

Sally sat at the bar, looking at her phone. *Where is this guy?* It was weird because when they spoke, he seemed genuinely interested and even eager to meet her. Harry said he didn't like texting and emailing, that he was old-fashioned and preferred to get together and talk like two human beings. Sally really liked that, but she also wondered if that was just some line. She wasn't born yesterday. She knew what men wanted. And yet Harry seemed different somehow, and even though that little voice in her head warned her that he's going to be like all the rest, she convinced herself to give this guy a shot. And now he's 15 minutes late. *Damn it. How could I be so stupid?!*

Well, given her track record, none of this surprised her. She had a special talent for picking losers. Five years ago, she discovered her husband was having an affair with her best friend. She found out by checking his phone, something she frequently did, and she never found anything…until she did. She was devastated, and yet it all seemed familiar. Her father wasn't a man of integrity either. He had an affair when she was 12 and left the family. That crushed her, but it nearly killed her mom, causing her to become depressed and a borderline alcoholic. To this day, Sally doesn't think her mom has ever truly recovered.

Sally never wanted that to happen to her, so in high school and college, she asked her friends to keep an eye on her boyfriends to make sure they weren't cheating. Years later, when the Internet and cell phones came along, she was able to keep an eye on things herself. And a lot of good that did her. Here she was, a 47-year-old divorced single mother of two with a history of being with untrustable men. And now she's sitting in some bar waiting to meet yet another guy she met online. *Why do I bother?*

Well, she knew the answer to that. After her marriage blew up, she swore off men for years and threw herself into her career and her kids. But, as Sally often sarcastically quipped, "men are like McDonald's French Fries: you know they aren't good for you, but you still want them." And on top of that, her youngest kid was going off college in the fall and even though her career kept her pretty busy, she was terrified of the "empty nest."

So, when Sally started dating again six months ago, she knew she had a wall around her heart, and she joked that every brick had some guys name on it. That wall was there to protect her from another jerk like her ex-husband. Men would have to prove that they were worthy of her trust before she'd ever take down that wall. And that included Harry. In fact, she was hoping they'd get into a conversation about their relationship histories because she didn't want to waste time on a guy who cheated in the past. *Once a cheater, always a cheater,* she mumbled under her breath. Just then, Harry walked up.

"Sally? Harry. Nice to meet you. Sorry I'm late. Traffic. Can I buy you a drink?"

INTRODUCTION

Fit to Be Tied

"Your task is not to seek love, but merely to seek and find all the barriers within yourself that you have built against it."

~ Rumi

13th Century Mystic Poet

Imagine that I am a former world-class triathlete. Back in my prime, I competed in and frequently won triathlons all over the globe, including the famous Ironman Triathlon in Hawaii. But since I am older now and retired from competition, I use my experience to coach others on how to be successful in triathlons.

And that's why you've called me. You are going to participate in an Ironman Triathlon and you don't want to just finish the race, you want to do really well. So, you're requesting a coaching session because you have a bunch of questions and you're hoping I can help. Well, I can, and because you're obviously committed to being successful (which makes you my kind of client), we make an appointment to meet and talk.

A couple of days later you're sitting in my office firing questions at me, one after another. It's so much fun. I love your enthusiasm and eagerness to learn. You ask questions about what you should eat before and during the race, and you ask how much water you should drink and when. You ask about the frenzied start and how to steer clear of the initial madness in the water when everyone is flailing away, jockeying for position. You want to know how to successfully navigate the critical transitions from swimming to biking to running. And you ask all kinds of questions about the course itself, where to slow down and conserve energy, and when to pick up the pace and make up time. On and on you go.

But after a while, I notice something that concerns me. There's a theme to your questions. *They're all about the actual race.* You're asking "race day" questions. You're asking about strategy and tactics, what to do and what not to do—*during the race.* And while those are important questions, in my experience as a former world-class triathlete, those are not the questions you should be asking.

You should be asking about how to train and prepare for the race.

That's a far more important issue. Are you fit enough to swim 2.4 miles, bike 112 miles and run 26.2 miles—consecutively, without stopping? Is your body prepared for such a grueling test of endurance? But you're not asking about that. You're asking about the actual race, and that is a huge mistake. So, finally, I interrupt you.

"Hey, the questions you're asking are about the actual race, and at some point, they are worthy questions to be discussed. But I don't think they are the questions you should be asking right now. In my experience, you should be asking about how to train and prepare for the race. In other words, you should be asking *training* questions, not *racing* questions. If you're not physically prepared for the race, if you're not in shape, what good will it do to have the perfect race-day strategy? Do you understand?"

You nod, and so I continue.

"Now, you've hired me to be your coach and I need to be honest with you. From what I can tell, you don't seem physically fit enough to finish even the swimming portion of the race, much less the whole thing. Frankly, it looks to me like you are 20-30 pounds overweight and there's no way you're ready for what's ahead of you."

My directness stuns you, but because I want to help you so much, I won't back down.

"I don't think you have any idea how difficult a triathlon is. It's probably the hardest thing you're ever going to attempt in your life. So, forget about all the race-day questions. That's not where your focus needs to be. It's about your fitness. It's about training. It's about being prepared for race-day."

I can tell you're discouraged.

"Having said that, I love that you want to do this! It's such a great goal. And you can do it and I definitely want to help you. Finishing that race and being declared an "Ironman" is one of the best feelings you'll ever have in life. Trust me, I've done it and it's worth the effort. But you have to work on yourself. You have to get prepared. You have to train. You have to get in the best shape of your life! And it's not going to be easy. But if you're willing to work hard, then you've come to the right place."

RACE-DAY

While I'm not a triathlon coach, I am a relationship coach, and what I just described is *exactly* the situation I encounter with my clients nearly every day. They come to me because they want to attract a fulfilling, lasting intimate relationship and they have a bunch of questions about how to do that. And that's fine. I love that conversation.

But they make the same mistake our aspiring triathlete did: They ask "racing" questions when they should be asking "training" questions.

For example, I am constantly asked about where to go to meet people, how to approach them in public (or how to get them to approach you), and I'm asked about how to start a conversation. I'm asked about flirting, chemistry and how to determine compatibility. And while those are valid questions that need to be addressed at some point, they are "race-day" questions, and therefore, they aren't the questions you should be asking.

When a triathlete stands on the starting line, if they're not physically fit, it's too late. They are going to fail. It's guaranteed. It doesn't matter how good their strategy is. If they're not in shape, they won't go the distance.

The same is true in our love lives.

The starting line for relationships is that moment when you come face-to-face with a potential mate. They're standing right in front of you. This might happen when you "swipe right" or when you meet someone from Match.com or when you're out with friends or when you're fixed up by a co-worker. It can also happen in the normal course of life, like when you're waiting for your luggage at the airport, or attending a networking function, or, as it was in my case, when you're sitting next to someone at a conference.

When this moment comes (and it will), when you're standing right in front of a potential partner, if you're not relationally "fit," you are going to fail just like an out-of-shape triathlete would. You are not prepared to create a healthy, conscious, sustainable relationship. It won't matter if you have a great "race day" strategy, you won't be able to "go the distance."

Granted, if you do focus on "race day" strategies, you might get a few dates. But, frankly, anyone can do that, just like anyone can start a triathlon. But starting isn't the issue, finishing is. And the same is true in your love life. *The issue is not can you start a relationship, the issue is can you finish one.* If you're not relationally "in shape," even if you meet a great person, you won't be able to go the distance.

GETTING READY FOR SOMETHING REAL

Getting ready for something real—a relationship that will go the distance—is what this book is all about. We're going to get you in tip-top relationship "condition." This is not about getting "toned," it's about getting "ripped." In other words, this book is not about how to create a decent relationship, one where you get along and don't want to kill each other. No, this book is for people who want the absolute bliss of authentic, conscious intimacy. And furthermore, it's for those who want it so much that they're willing to engage in some hard-core training to get it.

And make no mistake about it, hard-core training is needed, because attracting and sustaining a healthy relationship with another human being is far more difficult than finishing a triathlon.[1]

DO YOU NEED RELATIONSHIP BOOTCAMP?

Now, it might be unfair of me to assume that you are relationally "out of shape," and "20-30 pounds overweight." (I admit I am assuming that.) It is possible that you don't need *hard-core training*. Perhaps a little "toning"—a couple of forward bends and some "down-dogs"—will do. OK, fair enough.

What I can tell you is that when I finally took an honest look at my love life, I had to admit that I was significantly "overweight." In fact, I wasn't just a little "chubby," I was "morbidly obese" and my relationship history showed it. I had been through a divorce, I'd been dumped by my fiancée, and I had bunch of internet relationships that were filled with spectacular and embarrassing amounts of drama.[2]

I needed hard-core training in the worst way and so I hired a relationship coach who put me through the very "workouts" I'm going to take you through. And because I was deeply committed to working on myself, I got "in shape." And my hard work enabled me to attract and create a wonderful, conscious relationship with my wife and we show no signs of slowing down.

But the question remains: Do *you* need hard-core training? Well, if you can relate to "Harry" or "Sally" in the prologue, if you share any of their fears, frustrations or feelings, then the answer is absolutely *YES!* you need this book. While those two are dealing with some very common and normal

---

[1] 90% of those who start an Ironman Triathlon finish, while only 44% of those who start a marriage finish.
[2] If you think I'm exaggerating, read my first book, *A Drink with Legs.*

issues, they are in no "condition" to create a healthy relationship with each other or with anyone else for that matter.

But if you need more convincing, here are a series of True/False questions that are designed to help you determine your level of relational fitness.[3] And—*spoiler alert!*—if you answer "True" for any of them, you need this book. (Full disclosure: they were all true of me at one point in my journey.)

_____ Being single is not OK with me. It's a problem that needs to be fixed.

_____ I have a list of qualities I want in a partner.

_____ I've been hurt before, and consequently, I have some "trust issues."

_____ I feel lonely at times and I think finding the right partner would fix that.

_____ I've experienced some sort of repeating and painful pattern in my love life.

_____ In relationships, sometimes I know I need to speak up, but I'm afraid that doing so might make things worse or even chase the other person away.

_____ While I'm not perfect, the problems in my past relationships were caused mostly by my partners and their issues.

_____ I've had 2 or more long-term (more than a year) relationships that have not gone the distance.

---

[3] To receive a free, thorough and confidential assessment of your relational fitness level, visit https://coachingwithroy.com/the-relationship-fitness-self-test/ There you will find a detailed questionnaire that will not only evaluate and *score* your level of relational "fitness," but it also offers personalized recommendations based upon your score.

_____ Words like "vulnerability," "surrender" and "trust" are really scary ideas for me.

_____ I fear rejection and I lack confidence to such an extent that I rarely walk up to a stranger and say "hello."

_____ I sometimes worry that I might never meet someone special.

_____ I believe in the Law of Attraction and I want to use it to attract my life partner.

_____ I have been told I'm intimidating and too self-sufficient.

_____ I feel obsessed with finding a relationship and feel empty without it.

_____ I believe that the purpose of a relationship is to meet each other's emotional needs.

_____ I believe that to find a person with whom I feel both chemistry and compatibility is like finding a needle in a haystack.

_____ I am a little scared of intimacy, which is why I probably have "commitment issues."

_____ I have been told that I'm either clingy and needy or that I'm distant and emotionally unavailable.

_____ My past relationships have been painful, and I believe that opening my heart means opening to pain. If I'm honest, I'm not sure I want to take the risk.

_____ I believe that trust has to be earned and that it's based upon the other person's character and behavior.

THE INSIDE-OUT APPROACH

Now that we've established that you are probably at least a little bit "out of shape" (relax, nearly everyone is), we can now get specific about relationship "fitness." What exactly does that mean? Well, creating a beautiful, healthy relationship is a lot like how we would create a beautiful, healthy body. The similarities are quite astonishing.

For example, if you want a beautiful, healthy body, it will be **the result of,** or a **reflection of,** your understanding and dedication to seven things: (1) strength training, (2) aerobic conditioning, (3) core stability, (4) flexibility, (5) nutrition, (6) hydration and (7) rest.[4] Likewise...

If you want a beautiful, healthy, intimate relationship, *that* will be the result of, or a *reflection of*, your understanding and dedication to seven profound relationships—*going on inside of you*—right now.

Right now, in this very moment, you **are** in a relationship; in fact, you are in seven of them! I don't care if you're single. I don't care if you don't have any friends. Hell, I don't care if you're Tom Hanks in *Cast Away*, stuck on a deserted island and your only friend is "Wilson" (a volleyball)! *The fact is you are in seven relationships right now and they are all happening inside of you.*

These seven inner relationships are far more important than any outer relationship could ever be because the inner relationships determine the quality and sustainability of the outer relationships. Any outer relationship you have, intimate or otherwise, is the **result of,** or a **reflection of,** these seven inner relationships. And to the degree that these seven inner relationships are healthy, your love life will be healthy, but to the degree that they're dysfunctional, your love life will be dysfunctional.

---

[4] While I don't have a degree in exercise physiology or sports medicine, it seems to me that these seven issues represent what it means to be physically fit. If you're an expert in such things, forgive me if I've left something out.

OUR BIGGEST MISTAKE

The biggest mistake we make in our pursuit of intimacy is putting all of our attention on the outer relationship. We focus on finding "the one" and attracting our "soulmate." We use the Law of Attraction and make a list of qualities we want in a partner. We "swipe," we speed date, and we scour online profiles looking for a partner. We concern ourselves with where to meet *them*, how to approach *them*, what to say to *them*, how to flirt with *them*, and how to get a date with *them*. That's where our attention is—on ***THEM***. And that is a huge mistake because the quality of any intimate relationship is the result of, or a reflection of, what's going on inside of ***US***.

This book is an invitation to change your focus. As strange as it sounds, if you want to experience a great relationship, you have to stop focusing on THEM and how to find THEM, and instead focus squarely on YOU, because...

No intimate relationship will ever be healthier than you are.

PREVIEWING THE "WORKOUTS"

Therefore, *Relationship Bootcamp* consists of seven hard-core "workouts," each one focusing on one of the seven *inner* relationships (or "major muscle groups," if you will). And what you will quickly see is that these *inner* relationships are very deep and complex. Therefore, our goal is not perfection or complete mastery. You just need these seven inner relationships to be "stronger" than they are now (perhaps a lot stronger). So even though you will be required to work really hard on yourself, this is about progress, not perfection.

Having laid that groundwork, here is a short preview of the seven "workouts":

Workout #1: Strengthening your relationship to *REALITY*

This section looks at three realities: your relationship status, your true motivations and your relationship results. Do you relate to these realities from a place of acceptance and trust or from resistance and judgment? Your attractiveness is determined by this most fundamental relationship of all, the one you have to reality.

Workout #2: Strengthening your relationship to your *MIND*

Do you listen to "the voice in the head" and believe what it says, or do you laugh at it and ignore what it says? If you don't understand how your mind works and learn to question the stories it tells, you will never be happy in a relationship.

Workout #3: Strengthening your relationship to *FEELINGS*

Do you welcome, learn from and release your feelings and emotions, or do you withhold, suppress or apologize for them? What do you do when you're an emotional wreck? Learning to be emotionally intelligent is critical if we want to be happy and relate in a healthy, sustainable way.

Workout #4: Strengthening your relationship to the *PAST*

One of our favorite hobbies is collecting bad experiences. Yet, if we don't learn to let go of our "baggage," if we keep it alive in us, we will never live and love with an open, available heart, which is absolutely essential in our pursuit of intimacy.

Workout #5: Strengthening your relationship to your *TRUTH*

We all have thoughts, feelings, fears, desires and experiences. That is our truth. The issue is, what do we do with it? Do we reveal it and make ourselves known, or, because of fear and shame, do we conceal it and hide from the very people that matter to us?

Workout #6: Strengthening your relationship to your *ENERGY*

If we aren't feeling alive, joyful, passionate and "in the flow," it's because we're energetically blocked. Our "hose" is kinked, you could say. These blocks not only sap our aliveness, but they diminish the power of our masculine presence or our feminine radiance, which is the key to healthy chemistry and intimacy.

Workout #7: Strengthening your relationship to *LOVE*

Are you obsessed with finding love or do you fear it? Do you feel empty and lonely without love, or do you equate it with pain, or with losing yourself, or with being controlled? What does love mean to you and what stories do you hold about it?

GETTING THE MOST OUT OF THIS BOOK

Do you see what I mean about these being deep and complex issues? Wow, right? Yet, in one single book, we are going to get you "stronger" in all of them! That's quite a challenge, and it won't happen unless you do the following four things:

First, spend significant time on each section, perhaps months. Don't read this like a normal book. Don't rush through it. This book is not intended to be a "page-turner." *I want it to stop you dead in your tracks.* Take the "crock pot" approach. Let the ideas "slow-cook" and "simmer" within you. Wonder about them. Sit with them. Meditate on them.

Secondly, almost every chapter has a special application section called, **WORKOUT!** This is where I invite you to do practical exercises or answer questions that are designed to get you "in shape." If you want this book to change your life, *then do these "workouts."*

Third, whether you're reading the paperback or the e-version, **get a journal.** Many of the "workouts" require quite a bit of reflection and you'll want to record your insights in a separate place.

Lastly, reach out to me if you need help with any of the seven inner relationships that are discussed. When I first worked on these issues in my life, I needed the guidance and support of a coach, and you might too. So, I am available to work with you directly. But I also offer online group-training programs called, *Online Relationship Bootcamps.*[5] They are a fantastic (and less expensive) way to get in the best relationship shape of your life.

A FINAL WORD

The purpose of this book is to completely overhaul your way of being in the world. It's designed to shift your very DNA, inviting you to live and love in a completely different way. To do that, I'm going to present some truly outrageous and radical ideas, and I'm concerned that you might dismiss them if you thought they came strictly from me. *They most certainly have not.* While I have been doing the seven "workouts" for years and have become pretty "strong" as a result, these ideas have not originated with me. They've come from ancient masters like Buddha and Jesus, as well as from some of the more important spiritual teachers of our time, people like Michael Singer, Eckhart Tolle, Byron Katie, David Deida and Jim Dethmer to name just a few. I quote people like that throughout the book to help you trust and embrace the radical nature of what's being presented and not reject it as merely "Roy's wild-ass ideas about life, love and the pursuit of intimacy."

---

[5] For info see: www.coachingwithroy.com or email me at coachingwithroy@gmail.com.

LET'S BEGIN!

Ok, are you ready to "workout"? Warm up a bit, do a little stretching and be sure to have a water bottle and a towel handy because the first workout is going to kick your ass!!

WORKOUT #1

STRENGTHENING YOUR RELATIONSHIP TO REALITY

RESIST or ACCEPT

Chapter 1: Reality & Your Relationship Status

Chapter 2: Reality & Your Pursuit of Intimacy

Chapter 3: Reality & Your Relationship Results

"The truth is, everything will be okay as soon as you are okay with everything. And that's the only time everything will be okay."
~ Michael Singer

— 1 —

REALITY

&

Your Relationship Status

"This is the day the Lord has made; let us rejoice and be glad in it."
~ Psalm 118:24

Let's begin with a number of really stupid questions:

Would you be more attracted to: (A) someone who is happy being single, joyfully living their life and trusting that everything is occurring perfectly, or (B) someone who feels being single is a problem, and therefore, needs to be in a relationship?

Would you be more attracted to: (A) someone who is grateful for every relationship experience they've had and trusts that all future relationship experiences will be exactly what they most need for their growth, or (B) someone who is bitter, guarded, suspicious and untrusting?

Would you be more attracted to: (A) someone who shows up authentically and openly—without trying to be liked—and is genuinely curious about who you are, or (B) someone who sees dating as a kind of "job interview" where they evaluate you and/or try to "sell" themselves?

Would you be more attracted to: (A) someone who simply enjoys your presence and the opportunity to get to know you, without trying to size you up, or (B) someone who has a list of qualities they want in a partner, and then asks questions trying to find out if you meet them?

Would you be more attracted to: (A) someone who wants to make themselves known by candidly revealing their true thoughts, feelings and desires—no matter the risk, or (B) someone who "plays their cards close to their chest" in an effort to not scare you off and control your impression of them?

"B" STUDENT?

Those really *are* stupid questions, aren't they? The answers are obvious. No one is drawn to the "B" attitudes and perspectives. They're a turn-off. The energy motivating those behaviors isn't sexy or attractive—not to you, not to me, not to anyone. But here's where this first "workout" starts getting tough. Are you willing to admit that you share some, *if not all,* of the "B" perspectives? Aren't you a "B" Student? (Come on now, we aren't going to get anywhere unless you're honest with yourself.)

I realize that I've used very strong and unflattering phrases in the "B" category. No one wants to think of themselves as being lonely, needy, guarded, scared, suspicious or controlling. But the truth is, 99% of us are "B" people. I certainly was, and there's no shame in this. There's nothing wrong with being a "B" type person, *except that it's a very unattractive way of being in the world.*

"A" people, however, are beyond attractive—*they're irresistible!* Go back and read the "A" statements again. Who doesn't want to be with a person like that? "A" people are joyful, trusting, open, passionate, authentic, playful and fearless, and consequently, *they are the most attractive people in the world.*

Being relationally "in shape" means being a "A" person, and when you're in that kind of "condition," people will line up around the block to be your partner.

GETTING STRONGER

The way you become that attractive and irresistible "A" type person is by strengthening your relationship to REALITY. All the "B" perspectives reveal a very weak relationship with reality, while the "A" perspectives reveal a very strong one. But let's back up a minute. What do I mean by "your relationship to reality"? That's a strange phrase, probably one you've never heard of before, so let's start with a definition.

Reality is what's occurring right in front of you (or within you) right NOW. Reality is the suchness of this present moment. In other words, reality is—*what is.*

The issue is, how do you feel about reality, about—*what is?* What is your relationship to NOW? Do you love it or hate it? Do you welcome what's unfolding right in front of you (or within you) or do you reject it? Is reality a problem or is it perfect? Is it your ally or your enemy? In other words,…

Is your relationship to reality one of acceptance or resistance?

It's easy to fool ourselves on this, so let's do a quick reality check:

- It's your wedding day and you've planned an outside ceremony, and it's pouring down rain. Is your relationship to *this* reality one of acceptance or resistance?
- You're running late, and you're stuck behind a car that's going 45mph in the left lane. In *this* NOW moment, are you stressed or surrendered?
- You're looking down at the number on your bathroom scale, or at the number in your checkbook, or at the date of birth on your driver's license. Do you love *what is* or hate it?

- Your boss says, "I have to let you go," or your doctor says, "I found a dark spot on your x-ray," or your partner says, "I don't love you anymore." Are you in a place of acceptance or resistance?
- You're experiencing loneliness or anxiety or stress or sadness or boredom or frustration or hurt. Are those feelings welcomed as your ally, here to teach you something, or are they rejected as your enemy, here to make your life miserable?
- You're single. That's your current relationship status. It's *what is*. How do you feel about that? Is it a problem to be fixed or is life perfect as it is?

What you're going to find (and you might see this already) is that you live in an almost constant state of resistance.[6] That might show up as being angry or depressed about what has happened in the past, or it might show up as being worried and anxious about what might happen in the future. But mostly, it shows up as not being OK with NOW. Usually, there's something wrong with *what is*, with this present moment. Whether it's people, circumstances or conditions, life shouldn't be the way it is. **This** is not OK. **This** is not right. **This** is certainly not perfect. Resistance means you're at war with life and your experience of it.

THIS IS THE DAY…

If you see being single as a problem that needs to be fixed, you're resisting reality. This NOW moment, being single, is not OK. In fact, it's far from it. For you, this is a problem. You don't want to be single and something needs to be done about it.

---

[6] You're not alone, for I often do too. While I have come a long way, I don't want to give the impression that I'm some sort of enlightened being. I'm just "one beggar telling other beggars where to find bread."

But notice the attitude expressed in the quote that opened this chapter. The Psalmist wrote, *"This is the day the Lord has made; let us rejoice and be glad in it."*[7] That is what acceptance looks like. And make no mistake: the phrase, "this is the day," it's not referring to the day you go to your church, temple, mosque or wherever you go to connect with the divine. "This is the day" means *this moment*. It means NOW. It's referring to *what is*. And the Psalmist's attitude toward reality is one of joyful acceptance, not one of frustrated resistance.

"This day" is not a problem to be fixed but a moment to be trusted and enjoyed.

Furthermore, "this day" is occurring by divine design, for it's what "the Lord has made." Whether you call it God, Source, The Universe, The Quantum Field, or Life (as I do), the teaching is that reality is not an accident. It's the manifestation of divine intelligence.

SCIENCE vs. SPIRITUALITY?

However, this perspective is not at odds with science. Although spirituality and science explain reality from different perspectives, they, in fact, *arrive at the same conclusion.* Spirituality says that "this day" is created by the divine. Science says that "this day" is the result of all the forces that have created it, i.e., physics, chemistry, biology, psychology, etc. So, it doesn't really matter whether your perspective is spiritual or scientific, for as Michael Singer says, "all that matters is that you know that you didn't create it."[8]

---

[7] I am well aware that the Bible is a very polarizing spiritual text, but when it (or any ancient spiritual text) has something valuable to say, as it does here, I'm going to quote it and hope that you can receive its wisdom without thinking I'm promoting any particular religion, nor trying to convert you to anything. Know that I do not identify with any particular religion, but I do find value in some aspects of almost all of them.

[8] Michael Singer is my favorite spiritual teacher. Each time I quote him, and it happens frequently, it comes from either his extraordinary book, *The Untethered Soul* (the best spiritual growth book ever written, in my opinion) or directly from one of his talks.

Whatever we experience—people, conditions or circumstances—is unfolding impersonally. None of it is about us or caused by us. It's just *what is.* And yet we get to interact with it, and that interaction can come from a place of acceptance and trust or from resistance and judgment. So, it doesn't matter whether you're spiritually or scientifically inclined (or both, as I am). Reality is reality. It only matters how we choose to be with it.

And when we choose to resist rather than accept our relationship status, it means being single sucks! *"It shouldn't be this way. It's not OK that I'm single and it's certainly nothing to be "glad" about. It's a damn problem that needs to be fixed."* This kind of resistance is sabotaging your love life because…

Wanting a relationship is the very thing that is keeping you from having one.

Krishnamurti, a great Indian spiritual teacher from the 20th century, was once asked to explain why he was so peaceful and content. He simply said, *"I don't mind what happens."*[9] That means he didn't want life to be different. He had no argument with reality, no resistance or judgment of it. He was OK with however life unfolded. And this way of being in the world is not some unattainable state that is reserved for people like the Psalmist, Michael Singer or Krishnamurti. We, too, can face reality and "rejoice and be glad in it."

It's a choice.

When we find ourselves resisting and arguing and fighting with reality, whether it's with the traffic, our checkbook or our relationship status, we can shift by taking a deep breath of acceptance and say, *this is the day the Lord has made. I will rejoice and be glad in it.* And when we clench up again in

---

[9] This story is told in Eckhart Tolle's great book, *A New Earth.*

resistance (as we surely will), when we drift back into minding what's happening, we can shift again…and again and again.

Shifting your relationship to reality is not a one-time thing. It's done moment-to-moment, day after day until it eventually becomes your normal way of being in the world, until you can say from your heart, *I don't mind what's happening.*

"The most important, the primordial relationship in your life is your relationship with the Now, or rather with whatever form the Now takes, that is to say, what is or what happens. If your relationship with the Now is dysfunctional, that dysfunction will be reflected in every relationship and in every situation you encounter."
~ Eckhart Tolle [10]

NOT A PRETTY PICTURE

Now, if you think this is just some silly philosophical discussion that has no practical application for your love life, you couldn't be more wrong.

Your relationship to reality determines your relationship status.

How so? Well, allow me to paint a picture of what happens when you mind being single. It's not a very pretty picture, to say the least, but I know from personal experience that everything I'm about to say is absolutely true.[11] You will exhibit at least six very unattractive attitudes and actions if you believe being single is a problem that needs to be fixed.

1. **You'll be obsessed with finding a partner.** You will devote an enormous amount of time, attention, energy and money to fixing

---

[10] Every time I quote Tolle, and it happens frequently, it comes from either *The Power of Now* or *A New Earth.*
[11] My first book, *A Drink with Legs*, graphically describes how I did everything you're about to read.

this problem, and consequently, other relationships in your life will "wither on the vine," so to speak. You won't put nearly the time or effort into yourself, your kids, your career or your friends as you normally would. When being single is painful, it's like having a migraine headache—you can't focus on anything other than making the pain stop.

2. **You'll be needy to some degree** (and any degree is unattractive). Loneliness and the fear of never finding someone will cause you to try too hard, come on too strong or move too fast. That energy will scare people away.

3. **You'll play games and be inauthentic.** Since you're not trusting Life and the way it's unfolding, you will believe that it's your responsibility to attract a partner and get them to like you. That will cause you to manage your image, hide your true feelings and pretend to be the person that you think they want.

4. **You'll try to change or control others.** When you meet someone who has potential, because you're not OK being single, you will try to change them into the person you need them to be so that they fully meet your criteria. You'll try to get them to lose weight or stop drinking or dress differently or want kids or go to church or get a higher paying job. And once you are in a relationship with them, you'll try to control them so that they stay being the person you need them to be.

5. **You'll compromise your boundaries, especially when it comes to sex and money.** In an effort to get someone to like you and secure a relationship with them, you might have sex before you're ready, or you might go to places you can't afford, or you might even give them money! Additionally, you may also overlook questionable behaviors or ignore "red flags" altogether.

6. **You'll experience anxiety constantly.** *"Do they like me?...Am I too old for them?...Do I make enough money?...Should I lose some weight?...Maybe I should get some "work" done...Can I trust them?...Am I going to get hurt?...Maybe I shouldn't have said that...What did they mean by that?...Why haven't they called?...What did I do wrong?"*

THAT'S HOT!

Isn't all of that sexy? Who wouldn't want to be in a relationship with someone like that? Obsessed, needy, inauthentic, controlling, willing to compromise their values and filled with anxiety. That's hot! Where can I find someone like that?

Everywhere.

And in the mirror.

I know that's really direct (and perhaps presumptive), but all of those things happen as a result of you simply resisting being single and seeing it as a problem that needs to be fixed.

SINGLE FOREVER?

Now, let me make something crystal clear. Accepting and surrendering to *what is* does not mean you're resigned to being single for the rest of your life, nor does it mean you sit at home waiting for someone to knock on your door. Quite the contrary.

You can still do everything you've always done, including dating online. You can still flirt, "swipe," go out with friends, attend speed dating events or ask to be fixed up.

Except that you do it for the pure enjoyment of the experience, and not because you need a specific outcome or result.

In other words, you drop your agenda for how things need to be, and instead, you trust in the wisdom of how Life is unfolding in this NOW moment. As Jesus said, *"Not my will be done, but Thine."*[12] From this perspective, you're not only OK with *what is,* but you're equally OK with *whatever will be.* You choose to trust the flow of Life, and you relax any effort to find or attract your partner. That is none of your business and it's not your responsibility.

Your responsibility is to respond to and interact with Life as it's currently unfolding, to be in harmony with *what is,* rather than being in an argument with it. If Life thinks that an intimate relationship is what's best for your life and growth, then you'll be in one. If not, you can trust that it's not what's best for you—in this NOW moment.

Again, that doesn't mean you're resigned to being single forever. It just means that you accept that you are NOW. You still live your life and do everything you want to do, but you do it with a heart that's wide open to, and at peace with, however life unfolds.

And when you're "in shape" like that, you'll be irresistibly attractive.

WORKOUT!

Before you go on to the next chapter, do the following short "workout." Take a moment (or a week!) and deeply sit with each of the following questions:

- Are you willing to make one of the following quotes your mantra, something you meditate on regularly and repeat to yourself constantly?
  - *This is the day the Lord has made; I will rejoice and be glad in it.*
  - *I don't mind what happens.*

---

[12] Luke 22:42

o *Not my will be done, but thine.*

- Are you willing to trust that Life is unfolding perfectly, that you're right where you need to be, having the exact experience you most need to have?

- Are you willing to see that reality is your ally, rather than your enemy, and consequently, are you willing to stop searching for love and start trusting in Life?

The Great Way is not difficult for those who have no preferences. When love and hate are both absent everything becomes clear and undisguised. Make the smallest distinction, however, and heaven and earth are set infinitely apart. If you wish to see the truth, then hold no opinions for or against anything. To set up what you like against what you dislike is the disease of the mind.

~ Seng Ts'an

Third Zen Patriarch, 606 AD

— 2 —

REALITY

&

Your Pursuit of Intimacy

"If you're looking for your ideal person, someone who meets your qualifications, you're ruining your love life and your relationships."
~ Michael Singer

One of my all-time favorite movie scenes is from *A Few Good Men*, where Jack Nicholson yells, "You can't handle the truth!"[13] Well, this chapter is going to present a truth that might be very difficult to handle. Not because it's complicated (it's not) but because it's *uncomfortable*. The truth I'm about to present in this "workout" exposes the true motivations behind our pursuit of intimacy and it's going to be really hard to swallow. So, let's begin with a simple question, although after you consider it, you'll find it's actually quite deep. The question is this:

Why do you want a relationship?

I know you're reading this book because you want to be in a loving, lasting intimate relationship, and that's fine…but why? Why do you want an intimate relationship in the first place? Well, some say it's because they desire companionship, or because they want to raise a family. For others, it's

---

[13] If you're not familiar with the scene, here it is: https://bit.ly/1f3C7Ae

having someone to lean on for support or having someone with whom they can share things in common. On and on we could go. There are as many answers to that question as there are people in the world, and you probably have your own. And whichever way you answer that question is fine. It's *your* truth.

But it's not *THE* truth.

Underneath all the surface reasons as to why we want an intimate relationship lies the REAL reason we pursue intimacy. **Though no one has probably ever pointed it out to you, there is a single and universal reason why human beings seek intimate relationships.** And unless it's understood, you'll struggle to ever experience a satisfying, sustainable relationship.

THE HUMAN CONDITION[14]

Now, to explain this *real* reason requires me to back up a bit and describe the human condition as a whole. In other words, if we look at it from a distance, what are we really up to when it comes to "life, love and the pursuit of intimacy"? Well, there are 5 realities concerning the human condition, and all of them can be verified by your own direct experience.

Reality #1:
You exist in there.

If I walked up to you and said, "Hello, are you in there?" what would your answer be? It's obvious, right? You're in there. You exist. You're a conscious, aware being.

---

[14] I learned this paradigm from Michael Singer.

Reality #2:
You're not OK in there.

What if I followed the first question with this one: "How are you doing in there?" How would you answer that? Well, you might reflexively say, "I'm fine" (as most of us do), but what's the truth? How are you *really* doing in there? In other words, what's it like to be you?

This is where the truth begins to get a little uncomfortable, because while it's OK in there sometimes, usually it's not, right? Usually there's some level of inner turbulence or unease going on inside. *Usually you're not OK in there.*

Now, I'm not saying you're always freaking out or that you're suicidal, but I am saying that peace and joy are, at best, very rare experiences. In other words, isn't something almost always bothering you? Aren't you frequently worried or frustrated or upset about something? (If you don't notice this, it's only because you've been feeling "not OK" for so long that "not OK" feels OK or normal.) But look closely and I think you'll answer "yes" to many of the following questions.

- Isn't it common to feel lonely, anxious, insecure or lost?
- Don't you often experience things like self-doubt, discouragement, boredom, regret or jealousy?
- Aren't you often stressed, overwhelmed, confused, tense or restless?
- Don't you frequently experience physical sensations like knots in your stomach, shallow breathing, tightness in your shoulders, tension in your neck or jaw, or heaviness in your heart?
- Don't painful memories or worst-case-scenario thoughts make it difficult to sleep, be alone or enjoy a quiet moment?

- Don't you have a voice in your head that is always rehashing the past or rehearsing the future, and then telling you that you're not good enough, or that you're unlovable, undesirable, unsafe or unworthy?

All of those are examples of being "not OK" in there. And aren't you feeling one (or many!) of those things pretty much all the time? If so, congratulations! You're human. Everyone feels these things, no matter what they say on Facebook. And none of it is wrong or bad. It's just reality. It's the human condition.

Spiritual teacher and author, Scott Kiloby,[15] puts it this way:

> "At the core of our experience is a deep restlessness that both propels us towards the future and makes the present moment feel threatening, as if we have to constantly escape it. Don't believe me though. Check it out in your own experience. Sit for two hours alone in a room without any of your usual addictive indulgences. This will bring up that core restlessness."

So, are we in agreement on the first two realities? That you're in there and that it's usually not OK in there? If so, we can move on to the third reality concerning the human condition, and this is where the truth gets really hard to handle.

Reality #3:
Your life's purpose is to fix that "not OK" feeling in there.

The feelings and experiences described in the bullet points above are so uncomfortable, and in fact, so *intolerable*, that our entire lives are devoted to

---

[15] *Natural Rest for Addiction,* by Scott Kiloby. He is a wonderful spiritual teacher and anytime I quote him it's from this book or one of the many one-on-one trainings I've had with him. You would do well to investigate his inquiry method called, *The Living Inquiries.* It is referred to in Appendix I.

fixing them. If your hand is on a hot stove, you'll quickly see that your life's purpose is to remove it. And if you feel lonely, unlovable, insecure or anxious, for example, your life's purpose will be to fix those feelings, because they are just as intolerable. Here's the truth about the human experience:

Every thought we have, every decision we make, every action we take, every goal we set, every hope and dream we imagine and every prayer we utter is ultimately about fixing some sort of "not OK" feeling on the inside.

Can you handle the truth?

The longer I pay attention to myself and the world around me, the more deeply I see how true this is. We are not seeking the *objects* of our affection (e.g., intimacy, money, beauty, fame, enlightenment or even God), we seek the *feeling* that we believe those objects will deliver. We believe those things will fix that "not OK" feeling on the inside and replace it with a feeling of aliveness, joy, peace or love.

Reality #4:
Your primary strategy for fixing that "not OK" feeling is to find an intimate relationship.

While some people seek money, beauty, fame, enlightenment or God, many people's favorite strategy for fixing their "not OK" feeling (certainly those reading this book!) is to find an intimate partner.

Remember our original question, *why do you want a relationship?* Now we have the most truthful answer. On the surface, we thought it might be about companionship, emotional support, or family, but in reality, when you wake up and see what's really going on, **the real reason we want a**

relationship is because we believe it will fix that "not OK" feeling on the inside.

I know this from personal experience. My painful relationship history forced me to take a cold, hard look at myself, and when I did, I discovered a truth so startling that it initially scared the hell out of me. *I realized that I needed the attention and affection of a beautiful woman to make me feel like a man.* (Translation: I needed a woman to make me feel OK on the inside.)

As I dug into my true feelings and motivations, I discovered that I was relying on an intimate relationship to do four things for me:

1. **Fill a void.** I felt empty and hollow when I wasn't in a relationship and I believed being in one would fill that void.
2. **Fix a problem.** I didn't like being single and I was afraid of growing old all alone. If I could find a woman, she'd fix that problem.
3. **Finish a story.** Growing up, I never felt desirable or wanted by women. My story was that I wasn't attractive enough. So, if I could attract a beautiful woman, that would put an end to that story.
4. **Find an identity.** For most of my life, I never felt good enough or special. But if I could be with a beautiful woman, that would make me "somebody," it would give me an identity.

Why do *you* want an intimate relationship?

Do you see that it's not really about companionship, family or emotional support, or whatever other reason you thought of when I first asked the question? Are you willing to own that it's really about something much deeper, perhaps something captured by one of the 4 F-phrases listed above?

WORKOUT!

Before we go on to the fifth reality, I have a short 4-step "workout" for you, one that will make this chapter truly transformational in your life. (Write your answers in your journal.)

Step #1: From the list of "F-phrases" above, I want you to pick the one that most closely describes your deepest relationship motivation. (Mine would be "finishing a story")

Step #2: A couple of pages back, I listed a bunch of bullet points that described a variety of "not OK" feelings and experiences. I want you to pick a single word (or phrase) from that list, one that best captures your most familiar "not OK" feeling. Feel free to come up with your own if it's not on my list. (Mine would be "feeling undesirable")

Step #3: Identify a specific behavior that you need your partner to do so that you don't have to feel your "not OK" feeling. Do they need to text you all the time, not look at other people, spend money on you, have sex with you, compliment you, listen to you, trust you, etc., etc.? In other words, what do you need from them in order to feel loved? (Mine would be "have regular sex with me")

Step #4: Insert all three of your answers into the following sentence (or rewrite it in your journal):

The *real* reason I want a relationship is to help me (insert your "F-phrase") _____ because I feel (insert your "not OK" feeling) _____. Therefore, I need my partners to (insert the needed behavior) _____.

As an example, here's what mine would look like:

"The real reason I want a relationship is to help me _finish a story_ because I feel _undesirable_." Therefore, I need my partners to have _regular sex with me._

The way you complete that sentence is the _real_ reason you want a relationship.

Say it out loud a couple of times and notice what happens in your body. Do you feel a space of acceptance open up inside or do you constrict in shame? Does your breath deepen or tighten? Does your mind relax or race? Just notice your reaction to the truth.

Now, in order to get us back on track, here's a summary of the four realities we've faced so far: (1) you live in there, (2) it's not OK in there, (3) your purpose is to make it be OK in there, and (4) you believe finding a partner is the best way to make it be OK in there.

This is the human condition. It's what we're up to. Everyone is doing it and none of it is wrong or bad. My only question is, _does it actually work?_ And that leads us to the fifth reality, the most important one of all.

Reality #5:
An intimate relationship will not fix that "not OK" feeling on the inside.

Ah, but conventional wisdom says it will. _If you're lonely, find a partner. If you feel unlovable, find someone to love you. If you feel undesirable, find someone who thinks you're sexy._ That makes perfect sense, doesn't it?
Except it doesn't work.

It's not a wrong strategy, it's just an ineffective one. A partner cannot fix that "not OK" feeling inside of you. In fact, nothing on the outside of you can fix something on the inside of you.[16] It just doesn't work that way. Believing a partner's love will fix that "not OK" feeling inside of you is like trying to paint a house with a hammer. It's not wrong, it just won't work! If you try, you'll be very frustrated and disappointed. Just as a hammer makes a lousy paint brush, so…

A Life Partner Makes A Lousy Life Source

But that's not what we hear from the world around us. Whether it's the media, movies, magazines or music, we are bombarded with the "you complete me" mindset.[17] We're told to believe in the power of a relationship to make us feel whole, complete and "OK" on the inside. For example, one of the most beautiful love songs ever recorded is, *At Last*, by Etta James. While I love the song, notice the "you complete me" message:

At last my love has come along,
my lonely days are over, and life is like a song.
At last the skies above are blue,
my heart was wrapped up clover the night I looked at you.
I found a dream that I could speak to,
a dream that I can call my own;
I found a thrill to press my cheek to,
a thrill I've never known.
You smiled, you smiled and then the spell was cast,
and here we are in heaven, for you are mine at last.

I know it's just a sweet love song, and perhaps I'm making too big a deal of it, but that's how we feel about relationships! We truly believe that a

---

[16] To make this point, Michael Singer playfully says, "If you eat a sandwich, I don't feel full."
[17] The "you complete me" mindset is fully explored in my first book, *A Drink with Legs*.

partner will end our "lonely days." In fact, we believe it's their job. It's our partner's job to love us in a way that fills our void, fixes our problem, finishes our story or helps us find an identity. And that list you have, the one that describes the qualities you want in a partner, *that's their job description!* (Can you handle the truth?) Your list describes exactly who your partner needs to be and how they need to behave so that you don't have to feel that "not OK" feeling of yours.

Good luck with that.

First of all, good luck finding a person who even wants such a job (would you?), and secondly, good luck finding someone who's capable of fixing that "not OK" feeling. No person is going to be able to consistently and adequately meet your emotional needs and keep you from feeling unloved, insecure or not good enough (or whatever your "not OK" feeling is). At some point, they'll fail at their job. Consider the following scenarios:

- What happens when your partner puts a lot of time and energy into their careers, friends or kids, and you're not their priority and focus? You'll feel unloved or lonely—again.
- What happens when your partner communicates with their ex, or hangs out with friends of the opposite sex, or notices a really attractive person, or doesn't respond immediately to your texts? You'll feel insecure or abandoned—again.
- What happens when your partner criticizes something you've done, or doesn't listen to you or take your advice, or fails to appreciate something you've accomplished? You'll feel unworthy, invisible or not good enough—again.

Life partners make lousy life sources. At some point they will fail to do their job and you will feel that old, familiar "not OK" feeling—again. And that's because you've tried to get someone "out there" to fix something "in here" and it doesn't work. Here's how spiritual teacher, Jeff Foster, puts it:

> "The truth is, if you are experiencing conflict in your relationships, you are likely seeking something from your partner without being aware of it. Seeking always leads to conflict of some sort, because in the end, you are looking for something the other person cannot give you. Unconsciously giving someone the power to complete you is the beginning of all the trouble. Nobody has the power to complete you. For the power that you are really looking for—the power of completeness, communion, intimacy—does not reside in someone else. The communion you seek is communion with life itself. What you really long for is a deep intimacy with your own experience—the deepest acceptance of every thought, every sensation, every feeling. And that cannot come from outside yourself."[18]

UNCONDITIONAL LOVE

Why is this such a big deal? Because three really awful things happen when we seek a relationship to fix our "not OK" feeling inside.

First, we'll never be happy with anyone. They will always disappoint us. Second, no one will ever be happy with us. The enormous pressure we put on our partners to complete us will push them away. Third, we'll be in drama all the time. When our partners fail at their job (and they will), we'll become critical and controlling in an effort to get them to commit or recommit to doing their job. Ugh, drama.

But when we let go of the "you complete me" mindset, something wonderful happens. We can actually love and—be loved—unconditionally! We can finally relate without requiring, demanding or expecting our partners

---

[18] *The Deepest Acceptance*, by Jeff Foster. It's one of the books I recommend in Appendix I.

to do things they are not capable of doing. Consequently, real *unconditional* love can finally be experienced, because...

> "Love asks nothing, needs nothing and requires nothing. It needs no response, no return and no reason. Love has no strings, it has no memory, it incurs no debt. It needs no vow, it needs no future and has no job description. If need exists, love doesn't. If seeking is present, love is absent. Love is not mutual. It is not a two-way street. It is freely given with no thought of return. Love, if it is actually love, is unconditional. Always."[19]

WHAT NOW?

So, where do these 5 realities leave us? Are we to conclude that human relationships are hopelessly self-centered and co-dependent? Are we to give up on them altogether? Heavens, no. The only thing we need to give up on is the idea that a relationship can and should fix that "not OK" feeling on the inside. That's no one's job but ours. Yes, we want to feel love, joy, peace and connection, but we need to recognize that it's not found in someone else's arms, but that it's found within ourselves. The shift is to stop *seeking* "out there" and start *sourcing* "in here."

And when we "source from within," we won't be disappointed, for as Jesus said, "the kingdom of God is within," and that from our innermost being flows "rivers of living water."[20] Every spiritual teacher from Buddha to Maharshi, to Singer to Tolle has said the same. That if we'll only look within, we'll find a felt sense of unconditional well-being right here, right now—and that's what the rest of this book is about.

---

[19] *A Drink with Legs,* chapter 6
[20] Luke 17:21 and John 7:38, respectively.

— 3 —

REALITY

&

Your Relationship Results

"The moment you realize that the way it is right now is the way you want it (usually on some unconscious level), you unleash a powerful force, the same power that will carry you to a new intention that has nothing—repeat, nothing!—to do with your past."

~ Gay Hendricks

Imagine that you're in a Hollywood movie, but just playing a bit part. You don't have the leading role or even a supporting one, nor are you the casting agent, the script writer or the director. You're just an actor in someone else's movie. As such, you don't get to choose who is in the movie with you, nor do you get to determine what they say or do. And you definitely don't have control over the plot and what happens in the movie— *because it's not your movie.* You're just playing a role in someone else's movie, so you don't have control over anything.

Can you picture that scenario? If so, now I want you to imagine the complete opposite situation.

It's the same Hollywood movie, only this time it's totally *your* movie. That means, first of all, that you have the leading role, but it also means you're the director, the script writer and the casting agent. In other words, you're in charge of everything. It's literally *your* movie. Therefore, not only do you have control over the plot and what happens in the movie, you get to choose your co-stars and tell them exactly what to do and say. In other words, you are in total control of absolutely everything.

Hold those two scenarios in your mind for a minute and let me remind you that in this section of the book, we're strengthening your relationship to REALITY. So, your first "workout" (Chapter 1) focused on the reality of being single. We saw that your choice was to either resist and hate *what is,* or to accept and trust how life is unfolding right now. One makes you unattractive, the other irresistible.

The second "workout" (Chapter 2) focused on the reality as to why you want a relationship in the first place. We saw that your choice was either to *seek* a relationship to fix that "not OK" feeling inside of you, or you could *source* those needs from within yourself.[21] One makes you needy and manipulative, the other sets you free to love unconditionally.

Now, this third "workout" focuses on your relationship results, the actual experiences you've had (and are having) in your love life. Who's responsible for them? This presents a mind-blowing choice. You can either *blame* other people and circumstances for your relationship results or you can take 100% *responsibility* for your experience. In other words, you can view your love life as if you're in someone else's movie, where things happen "to me" because you don't have control over anything, or you can view your love life as being *your* movie, where things happen "by me" because you are in control over what happens.

WHOSE MOVIE IS THIS?

So, how do you view your life? Are you in someone else's movie, or are you responsible for everything that has happened (or will happen) in your love life? You can either see yourself as a victim, believing things happen "to

---

[21] This theme will be revisited in Chapter 24.

me," or you can choose to see yourself as a creator, believing things happen "by me." What a radical question to consider! Does life happen "to me" or "by me"?[22] And here's the kicker: One answer keeps you single, the other leads to lasting intimacy.

Now, again, this may seem like another meaningless philosophical discussion that has nothing to do with your desire to attract a relationship. *But it has everything to do with it.* Let me explain how by asking you a very simple, straight-forward question:

Why are you single?

I actually want you to write your answer in your journal and be honest. *Why are you not in a relationship?* What's the reason? (Go ahead. I'll wait while you write it down.)

Now, look very closely at your answer, for it reveals how you truly view your life. Your answer, no matter what it is, will fall into one of two buckets: the "to me" bucket or the "by me" bucket. Let me help you identify which bucket your answer belongs in, for it's the key to attracting a satisfying and sustainable relationship.

Your answer belongs in the "to me" bucket if you *blamed* your relationship status on some issue, circumstance or person. (I'll give you a bunch of examples in a minute, but perhaps you can already see the blame in your answer, for 99% of all answers fall in this category.) Blame basically means you think you're in someone else's movie, that they (or it) wrote the script, and therefore, they (or it) are responsible for you being single.

Now, no one likes to see themselves as a victim. But if you aren't a victim, if you truly believed that life happens "by me," that it's *your* movie

---

[22] This little play on words, "to me—by me," is actually a part of a larger framework called *The Four Ways of Being in the World* (to me—by me—through me—as me). As far as I've been able to ascertain, it was originally developed by Michael Bernard Beckwith and then refined by Jim Dethmer and the Conscious Leadership Group.

and that *you're* writing the script, then your answer, whatever it was, would not have any blame in it. How could it, if you're in charge of the plot? Instead, you'd claim 100% responsibility for your relationship status, and your answer as to why you are single would sound something like this:

I am single because on some level I want to be single.
There must be some hidden benefit or payoff to being single, and in this moment, I claim 100% responsibility for my life and fully own that I am committed to being single.

IT'S *YOUR* MOVIE

Whoa, what an outrageous perspective! Claiming 100% responsibility for your relationship results (past, present and future) is crazy radical, but nonetheless, it's the truth. *It is your movie.* And although you probably don't see how or why the script you're writing calls for its star (you) to be single, the truth is you are committed to your life being exactly as it is. And we know this *because it's your movie.* It's not happening "to me," it's happening "by me." But that's not bad news; in fact, it's actually the best news ever!

For if you're writing the script (and you are) you can re-write it! If it's your movie (and it is), you can change the plot! When you shift from victim to creator, seeing that life happens "by me" rather than "to me," you empower yourself to write a completely different and happy ending for the star of your movie.

But if you blame your relationship status on some issue, circumstance or person, change becomes impossible. For if it's not your movie, then what can you do about it? Nothing. You're simply "at the effect of" whoever or whatever is in charge of the movie and what happens in it.

So, if you want to change the course and trajectory of your love life, if you want to re-write the script and create a happy ending for your movie, then the first step is to face REALITY. *You have to face the fact that you have seen yourself as an actor in someone else's movie.* Your "pursuit of intimacy" must start with this courageous admission. The first step is always admitting you have a problem.

So, in order to help you get absolute clarity on this most important issue, here is list of 25 different "to me" (victim) reasons people have for being single.[23] I wonder, do any of them resemble what you wrote in your journal a minute ago?

1. I just haven't met the right person yet. That's why I'm single.
2. All the good ones are taken or gay. That's why I'm single.
3. I won't go to bars or do online dating. That's why I'm single.
4. I'm picky. That's why I'm single.
5. I have emotional baggage from my past. That's why I'm single.
6. My work and travel schedule are crazy. That's why I'm single.
7. I'm too busy with my kids. That's why I'm single.
8. I've been married too many times and that scares people. That's why I'm single.
9. I've never been married and that scares people. That's why I'm single.
10. I have health or physical issues. That's why I'm single.
11. I'm too educated (or I never went to college). That's why I'm single.
12. I won't have sex right away (or until I get married). That's why I'm single.
13. I'm too tall (or short). That's why I'm single.
14. My career and financial situation are not good. That's why I'm single.
15. I don't know where or how to meet people. That's why I'm single.
16. I'm shy, quiet and introverted. That's why I'm single.
17. I'm not good at talking, flirting and creating chemistry. That's why I'm single.
18. There aren't many quality people where I live. That's why I'm single.
19. I'm intimidating because I'm so independent and self-sufficient. That's why I'm single.

---

[23] The list could be much longer, but 25 should allow you to get the idea.

20. I'm not attractive enough. That's why I'm single.
21. I'm overweight and out of shape. That's why I'm single.
22. I don't want kids, I do want kids, I have young kids, I have too many kids or I have special needs kids. That's why I'm single.
23. My personality is too quirky and different. That's why I'm single.
24. I'm taking care of my parents. Nobody wants to get involved in that. That's why I'm single.
25. I'm very conservative or liberal. That's why I'm single.

These are 25 different "to me" statements, ways we play the victim and blame our relationship status on some condition or circumstance. And here's the kicker: *not one of them is true.* They are all lies (as is any other reason you might come up with that's not on my list). However, don't misunderstand me. I'm not saying that, for example, you aren't picky. Maybe you are. Or perhaps you do have a crazy work schedule, or maybe you are independent and self-sufficient. I'm not saying that any of what's listed above is not a reality, ***I'm saying that none of them are the reason you're single.***

And I know this because there are millions of people with your very situation or circumstance, and they are in relationships! So why aren't you? And please don't say it's because you haven't met the right one yet. Hell, half the population is single. You are literally surrounded by wonderful and available single people every day and I'm pretty sure you're only looking for one. So, don't try to tell me you're a victim of fate, that the stars haven't lined up for you yet. No, it's your movie, *so the real reason you're not in a relationship is because on some level and for some unconscious reason, you don't want to be in one.*

"Until you make the unconscious conscious, it will direct your life and you
will call it fate."
~ Carl Jung

Now, that's a really hard pill to swallow, so let me clarify.

INTENTION VS. COMMITMENT

When I say you don't want to be in a relationship, I don't mean you
don't have a genuine intention to be in one. Of course, you do. What I am
saying is if it's not happening, and since this is your movie, then there's
some (unconscious) reason why you won't let yourself be with someone.
Yes, you have a surface *intention* to be in a relationship, but you must have a
deeper and stronger **unconscious** *commitment* to staying single (because it's
your movie).

And remember, unconscious commitments always win out over surface
intentions. Here's an analogy: The gas pedal in your car is like your
intention. You want to make your life go in a direction, so you press the
pedal. But an unconscious commitment is like having your other foot on the
brake at the same time. No matter how hard you hit the gas, your car will
make noise, but it won't move. That is exactly how it is in your love life.
You may make a lot of noise about how much you want to be in a
relationship, but if it's not happening, it's because your other foot is on the
brake.

**Therefore, the most important thing you can do for the future of
your love life is discover how and why you are committed to staying
single.** Once you do that, everything changes. This is exactly what Gay
Hendricks meant in the quote that opened this chapter:

"The moment you realize that the way it is right now is the way you want it (usually on some unconscious level), you unleash a powerful force, the same power that will carry you to a new intention that has nothing—repeat, nothing!—to do with your past."

What he means is that once you own that your foot is, indeed, on the brake, and deal with that, then your car will take off toward a relationship. But as long as your foot remains on the brake, you'll never let yourself be in a sustainable relationship.

And *sustainable* is the key word in that last sentence. If your foot is on the break, you'll still attract people, but you'll only attract people who are either incapable of making a commitment or those who simply have no interest in doing so.

EMOTIONALLY UNAVAILABLE

Have you ever wondered why you attract people who are married, separated or in the middle of a divorce? Or why you are a magnet for players, workaholics, alcoholics, or those who are hung up on an ex? Or why you are a sucker for "bad boys," the types that are attractive, but afraid of commitment and are emotionally unavailable?

Have you ever wondered why you wind up with those kinds of people? Well, now you know. They're safe. Those kinds of people fit with your unconscious commitment to staying single. The relationship can't go anywhere, and unconsciously, that is exactly what you want!

CURIOSITY & WONDER QUESTIONS

So, again, your love life literally depends on you being able to discover and dissolve your unconscious commitment to being and staying single. How do you do that? By becoming curious and asking wonder questions. And this happens quite organically, for if you truly believe that you've got your foot on the brake, you'll quite naturally want to know how and why.

But curiosity is not about figuring something out. Curiosity is a humble admission of ignorance coupled with an open-ended quest for self-awareness.

Curiosity is more of a spiritual practice done on one's knees, than an intellectual exercise done in one's head.[24]

Jim Dethmer, the co-author of *The 15 Commitments of Conscious Leadership*[25] puts it this way:

> "Wonder is a very different experience. It is not about figuring anything out. It begins with a willingness to explore and step into the unknown, which involves taking a risk and letting go of control—not an easy commitment. Once we're willing to be surprised by the unknown, the next step in accessing wonder is to ask a wonder question: an open-ended question that has no "right" answer."

WORKOUT!

This chapter's "workout" is to practice curiosity by asking wonder questions. What's listed below will help you begin the process of discovering your unconscious commitment to being and staying single. I invite you to approach them from a place of "contemplative curiosity." In other words, sit with them. Give them space and time. In my experience, it often takes weeks or even months for insight to emerge, so I encourage you to treat them like a mantra. Repeat them over and over again as you meditate or even when

---

[24] If you're going to pray about your love life, don't pray for a partner, pray instead for insight into your unconscious resistance to having one.

[25] *The 15 Commitments of Conscious Leadership*, by Dethmer, Chapman and Warner, is mostly written for business leaders, but its message equally applies to intimate relationships. Therefore, it is one of the books recommended in Appendix I and you are strongly encouraged to read it. Every time I quote Jim Dethmer it is from this book.

you're sitting in traffic. (Spiritual insight often occurs in the strangest places.)

- What are the downsides or the negatives to being in a relationship? Hmmm…
- What are the payoffs or benefits of being single? Hmmm…
- What might I lose or have to give up if I was in a relationship? Hmmm…
- What am I afraid would happen if I was in a relationship? Hmmm…
- What might it cost me if I was in a relationship? Hmmm…
- What am I doing (or not doing) to sabotage my love life? Hmmm…

WHAT'S NEXT?

I obviously don't know what answers will emerge as you sit with these wonder questions. But once the insights begin to come, and they will, you'll probably want to know what to do with them.[26] Here's what I can tell you for sure. Your curiosity quest is going to surface limiting beliefs and underlying fears. As long as you hold them to be true, as you are now, you will never allow yourself to be in a relationship (other than the kind that won't last). There's just too much risk.

These beliefs and fears have to be challenged because they control your behavior. The mind is really good at making up stories that are not true or that are based on the past. We have to learn how to handle that crazy storyteller that lives in our heads, and that's what the next section of the book is all about.

---

[26] This is where private coaching sessions become necessary. I'm ready when you are. My contact info is in this book but I can most easily be reached via email: coachingwithroy@gmail.com.

WORKOUT #2

STRENGTHENING YOUR RELATIONSHIP TO YOUR MIND

LISTEN or LAUGH

"We treat our minds like God or Guru, but it doesn't know anything! It's wrong all the time, yet we still listen to it. Ignore the mind as you would a financial advisor whose advice has always been wrong."
~ Michael Singer

— 4 —

MIND

&

Relationship Roles

"The most important relationship you have in your life is the one you have with your mind."

~ Michael Singer

Imagine that your best friend is very upset and needs to talk to you immediately. You can tell it's really serious, so you drop what you're doing and rush right over to see them. As soon as you arrive, they tell you what's going on and they start from the beginning:

"Many years ago, long before we met, I hired a relationship coach to help me attract a satisfying, sustainable relationship. And the coach I chose came highly recommended. In fact, everyone said they were the most trustworthy person for the job. So, I hired them and I'm still working with them to this day.

Never could I have imagined how awesome it would be to have a coach who not only cared about me but who was always available to help me make sense of dating and relationships. They promised to fulfill five important roles in my life.

First, my coach would serve as my *matchmaker*. They would tell me what qualities I should look for in a partner and then help me find them.

Second, my coach would serve as my *interpreter*. Whenever I felt confused or concerned about someone's words, actions or motives, they would interpret them, telling me what they meant.

Third, my coach would serve as my *Secret Service Agent.* They would search people's backgrounds, or at least scrutinize their behavior, and whisk me away to safety the minute anything suspicious happened.

Fourth, my coach would serve as my *psychologist.* If I met someone who, for example, wasn't close to their family, or had never been married, or had been abused in their past, they would diagnose the issue and tell me if I should run away or not.

Lastly, my coach would serve as my *psychic*. If I met someone that was recently divorced, or attended AA, or had an affair in the past, they would predict how that person would behave in the future, keeping me from making a huge mistake."

"Wow, your coach sounds incredible!" What's the problem, then? Why are you so upset?"

"Well, it does sound incredible, *except that almost every single thing they've told me has been wrong!* My relationship coach doesn't know what the hell they're talking about! All their advice has backfired, and my love life is a complete disaster.

For example, in terms of being a matchmaker, my relationship coach is pathetic at picking partners. The people they matched me up with turned out to be all wrong for me.

And as an interpreter, my coach is even worse. I once dated someone who was busy on the weekends. My coach interpreted that to mean they were married and told me to confront them about it. That blew up in my face, because not only were they not married, they dumped me because I had acted like such a crazy person. I often wonder what would have happened if I ignored my coach."

"What about the Secret Service thing? How'd that play out?"

"Oh my God, that was awful too! I met this one person online and they wanted to meet up right away. We went to a really nice place and we had such a good time that they wanted to see me again the next day—and then they tried to kiss me too! My Secret Service Agent coach told me they were coming on too strong and that they wanted only "one thing," so I never went out with them again. I wonder what might have happened, though, if I would have questioned my coach's judgment and gotten to know them better before walking away.

Oh, and then a little over a year ago, I met a really nice person. I mean, they were fantastic. We went out a few times and everything was great until I discovered that not only had they never been married, but they had never been in a committed relationship of any real length. Hearing that, my coach, the psychologist, told me to steer clear because they definitely had commitment issues. Then just last week, I found out they recently got married. Had I not listened to my coach, I might be married right now.

And if you think that's bad, my coach has a bunch of relationship philosophies, and they aren't opinions or stories either; my coach says they're *the truth*. For example, one of my coach's favorites is, "once a cheater, always a cheater." I can't tell you how many people I've blown off because I found out that they had cheated in their past.

Well, I was out with a group of people not long ago and I mentioned my coach's philosophy. You know, just making conversation. And most of them started laughing. Seems quite a few of them had cheated on a partner in the past and had never cheated on anyone since. What would have happened if I didn't listen to my coach's 'truth'?"

YOU'RE FIRED!

Now, again, imagine your friend telling you that story. What would your advice be? What would you say? Wouldn't you tell them to fire their coach immediately and not to listen to another word they had to say? Of course you would.

Well, I'm telling you to fire *your* relationship coach immediately and not to listen to another word they have to say either. What coach is that, you ask? The one that's living in your head. *Your mind is your inner relationship coach and it's been giving you horrible advice your entire life.*

Your mind should not be listened to; in fact, it should be laughed at.

Your mind thinks it knows everything and it doesn't. It thinks it's right about everything and it's not. It makes assumptions that cause you to misread situations, it projects its past on to others causing you to misjudge people, and it tells stories that cause you to misinterpret people's words, actions and motives. *Your mind is wrong all the time.* Have you noticed that? This is why Michael Singer playfully but seriously says:

"I'd rather listen to a Magic 8-Ball than listen to my own mind."

If you want to get "in shape" and experience a satisfying, sustainable, intimate relationship, then you must learn to not listen to your inner relationship coach, your Personal Mind.[27] **In fact, you must learn to be skeptical of its "advice," you must learn to question its "wisdom," and you must learn to distrust its "truth."**

Now, the suggestion to not trust your own thinking is quite radical, mostly because everyone tells you to trust yourself. But have you ever stepped back and examined your mind's track record? Have you ever given it a "performance evaluation?" In other words, has your mind done a good job as your relationship coach?

This is an incredibly important question, and to help you answer it, let's make a small change to the previous dialogue and see if it helps you understand just how untrustworthy your mind really is. Here is a portion of that dialogue, only this time, I've substituted "my mind" for "my coach."[28] I think you'll see it's an accurate description of your experience.

"…**[my mind]** is pathetic at picking partners. The people **[my mind]** matched me up with turned out to be all wrong for me. And as an interpreter, **[my mind]** is even worse. I once dated someone who was busy on the weekends. **[My mind]** interpreted that to mean they were married and **[my mind]** told me to confront them about it. That blew up in my face, because not only were they not married, they dumped me because I had acted like such a crazy person. I often wonder what would have happened if I ignored **[my mind]**…

Oh, and then a little over a year ago, I met a really nice person. I mean, they were fantastic. We went out a few times and everything was great until I discovered they had never been married…Hearing that, **[my mind]** told me to steer clear because they had commitment

---

[27] Other spiritual teachers call it "the voice in the head," "ego," "the personal self" or "the lower self." Regardless of the word or phrase, they all refer to the same thing.

[28] It would be quite tedious of me to do this for the entire dialogue, so I'm only making the switch for a portion of it. However, I strongly encourage you to go back in this chapter and do it for the entire dialogue. It makes it all the more powerful.

issues. Then just last week, I found out they recently got married. Had I not listened to **[my mind]**, I might be married right now."

The most important relationship in your life is the one you have with your own mind. If you listen to it, you're screwed. So, in this chapter, I'm going to put you through an outrageously challenging "workout." I'm going to show you why you should *not* listen to that neurotic "voice in the head," but instead, *why you should question and challenge every single thing that it tells you about "love, life and the pursuit of intimacy."*

THE UNTRUSTWORTHY MIND

The reason you shouldn't trust your mind is because its "wisdom" is based solely on what it has been exposed to and what it has experienced in the past—and nothing more. In a sense, your mind is like a computer which is also limited by its programming. For example, if you program a computer with data that says $2 + 2 = 5$, then every time you ask it what $2 + 2$ is, it's going to say 5. It can't say otherwise. And if you say, "Hey, computer, are you right about that?" it will emphatically say, "Hell YES!, I'm right." *And based upon its programming, the computer is right.*

This is why you feel *so* right about your beliefs and perspectives. They're based upon your mind's data, and from its perspective, it's right! But your mind's data is very incomplete. Case in point: if a woman has had 5 major relationships and each guy cheated on her, if you ask her mind if men are trustworthy, she'll emphatically say "Hell, NO!" And from her perspective, she'd be right. Men can't be trusted. *That's been her experience.* But there are billions of men on the planet and she's only been with 5 of them. So, when her mind tells her that "men can't be trusted," she'd be crazy to listen to that! In fact, she should laugh at it!

Right now, there are billions of things happening all over the planet and you aren't experiencing any of it. So, your mind's "wisdom" or "advice" is incredibly incomplete, and therefore, it's utterly untrustworthy. Yes, you've had a lot of experiences in your life—I have too—but in the grand scheme of things, it's a microscopic sliver of what's going on in the world. Therefore, how can you trust your mind when it gives you advice about men, women, dating or relationships?

A wise person is very skeptical about their mind's perspectives, so much so that they're open to the possibility that *the opposite of what they believe might be as true, or truer, than their mind's original belief.*[29] A wise person chooses to question their own thinking, they interrogate the "voice in the head," and they challenge what they believe is true because they understand that it's all coming from a ridiculously limited and incomplete perspective.

I'M RIGHT, YOU'RE WRONG!

But there's another dangerous dimension to this and it's truly an intimacy killer. When you take your mind's limited perspective to be the truth, you create the "I'm right, you're wrong" dynamic, and no meaningful connection can occur from that mindset. It is the basis of all drama and conflict, whether it's between religions, nations or lovers. But when you are humble enough to question your own convictions and perspectives, when you entertain the possibility that the opposite of what you believe might be true, you create a culture of curiosity, respect and true listening. These are the hallmarks of any healthy relationship, but they cannot exist as long as you listen to your mind and think you're right. Therefore...

A wise person values curiosity more than conviction.

---

[29] This is commitment #10 in, *The 15 Commitments of Conscious Leadership*, by Dethmer, Chapman and Warner.

ROLE PLAY

Having laid that groundwork, let's revisit the 5 roles we ask our "inner relationship coach" to play as we pursue intimacy.[30] My hope is that you'll see that it's not only silly to ask your mind to function in these ways, but it's truly dangerous and self-sabotaging to do so.

Matchmaker is the first role we ask our minds to fulfill. We ask it to identify the qualities we need in a partner and then we ask it to help us find such a person. This gets into the *Law of Attraction* and there are so many problems with it, that I'm using all of Chapter 6 to discuss it, so we'll wait until then.

Interpreter is the second major role we ask our minds to play. Since you are relating with people and not robots, it's inevitable that you will feel confused or puzzled by what others say or do. It just goes with the territory. That said, to feel confused or puzzled is very uncomfortable and scary, and your mind will attempt to make sense of it. In other words, in an effort to feel safe or in control, your mind will create a story to explain what's going on. It will interpret a person's actions, telling you what they mean. This is not wrong. It's just what the mind does when it's scared. However, how it does this is where you get into trouble.

The mind's only option to explain what's going on is to find a similar experience in the past and use it to explain the present. And the past event doesn't even have to be something you've personally experienced. It could be something a friend experienced or even something you read online or saw on TV. It doesn't matter. The mind is just looking for anything to help it make sense out of a confusing situation.

For example, let's say the person you're dating hasn't responded to a text message you sent hours ago. This is out of character for them, so you're confused and wondering what's going on. Instead of welcoming the

---

[30] There are many more, of course, but these five are the most popular (and the most destructive).

84

uncomfortable feeling of confusion and noticing where you feel it in your body and breathing with it as you relax, let go and move on with your day, your mind will try to fix that "not ok" feeling by explaining what their silence means, and it might go something like this: *Do you remember when 'so and so' broke up with you? The first thing they did was stop responding to your texts. So, wake up. You're about to get dumped!*

Now, if you listen to that and don't laugh at it, you'll do something you'll probably end up regretting. You might break up with them first, beating them to the punch, or you might blow up their phone insisting they tell you what's wrong, revealing the crazy person that lives in your head!

Bottom line: Your mind is a terrible interpreter and a great storyteller. Don't listen to it.

Secret Service Agent is the third role we ask our minds to play. Because most of us have been hurt in the past, we develop "trust issues," and our hearts become guarded and walled-off to some degree. The mind, then, functions as our "protection detail," standing between us and others, suspiciously scrutinizing everything they do and say, whisking us away at the first sign of trouble.

We will deal with the issue of the past in *Section Four*, but for now, all I want you to know is that in your desire to protect yourself, you're actually sabotaging yourself. People can feel your suspicion and your guardedness and it's a huge turn-off. They'll sense it in your overall attitude and presentation, and, of course, it will show up in the questions you ask.

But beyond that, there's an even more insidious dimension to this. *The mind has an unbelievable way of seeing what it wants to see.* Psychology calls it, "confirmation bias," and it's the tendency to search for or interpret information in a way that confirms one's preexisting beliefs or theories.

I described an example of this earlier. When you meet someone who is genuinely taken with you, they'll want to spend time with you, talk to you and even touch or kiss you. That's how people act when they really like someone. But if you've been deceived or "played" in your past, your "protection detail" will think they're coming on too strong, or that they only want "one thing" and it'll tell you to run for the hills. In other words…

Your mind will keep you safe, but it will keep you single.

This is not to say that you should ignore "red flags" or that you shouldn't have boundaries. It just means you have to be very careful of how your mind can see things that aren't there.

Psychologist is the fourth role we ask our minds to play. This one is a little like "secret service agent," except that rather than being suspicious of a person's motives or intentions, here your mind is suspicious of a person's mental or emotional health. And, again, in an effort to protect you, your mind is going to make up all kinds of stories about how some aspect of a person's past or personality makes them a poor choice as a partner.

For example, if you meet someone who had an alcoholic parent or was abused as a child, your mind might create a story that they have an abandonment or attachment disorder. If you meet someone who is not close to their family or who has never been married, your "inner psychologist" might make that out to mean they have intimacy or commitment issues.

Now, to be clear, I'm not saying those aren't possibilities. They might be. *But the opposite of those stories might be true, too.* That abused person might be the most solid, loving person you've ever met. And that person who's not close to their family might have good reason. (Maybe their family is filled with narcissistic control freaks!) And that person who's never been married might have consciously chosen that lifestyle for career reasons but is now ready for a relationship.

My point is you don't know. But if you listen to that "voice in the head," the one that thinks it knows everything, you might never give a particular person a chance and that could be a terrible mistake. So, wise up and don't listen to that psycho "psychologist" that lives in your head.

Psychic is the fifth role we ask our minds to play. Because the mind is so convinced that its beliefs, theories and philosophies are, in fact, true, it actually thinks it can predict the future behavior of others! The examples are endless, but here are a few:

- *Once a cheater, always a cheater. If they did it once, they'll do it again.*
- *If someone doesn't call you within 2 days of the first date, they're not interested.*
- *Men expect to have sex on the third date. If you don't, they'll bolt.*
- *Don't date someone who is recently divorced. They will eventually realize they aren't ready for a relationship and they'll dump you.*
- *People in A.A. will eventually fall off the wagon. They always do.*

On and on we could go. The mind is so terrified of the unknown that it will attempt to predict people's behavior so that it can feel safe and in control. And if it has to make stories up, it will!

In the end, your mind is your worst enemy. Though you think it's trying to help you, it's actually sabotaging your love life and ruining your chance at intimacy.

Don't listen to it; instead, laugh at it.

"One day you may catch yourself smiling at the voice in your head, as you would smile at the antics of a child. This means that you no longer take the content of your mind all that seriously."

~ Eckhart Tolle

WHAT'S NEXT?

The question you are probably asking at this point is, if my mind is an untrustworthy source of wisdom and guidance, then how do I function in my love life (or life in general)? Wouldn't I be a ship without a rudder if I don't rely on my own thinking? How would I pick a partner or how would I know if I'm a good fit with someone if I don't use my mind? How would I know if I should go on a second or third date or break it off? How am I supposed to handle confusing situations or know when to become exclusive or when to have sex? Don't I need wisdom and guidance in my pursuit of intimacy?

Yes, you absolutely do. But not the wisdom that comes from what we've been discussing in this chapter, not from what I call your **Personal Mind**. In the next chapter, we're going to explore a deeper, more trustworthy source of wisdom, something that's far more intelligent, something I call, **Presence Mind.**

WORKOUT!

But, before we get to that, let's do a really difficult "workout." This is an important part of getting in "relationship shape," so take as much time as you need and breathe as you do this.

For each of the four roles discussed in this chapter,[31] answer two questions: First, how has that role shown up in your life, and secondly, what has it cost you? In other words, give me an example of each role and tell me

---

[31] Remember, "Matchmaker" will be dealt with in Chapter 6.

the consequence of listening to it. What might have happened (or not happened) had you not listened to your mind in that way? Write your answers in your journal.

Interpreter
- An example of my mind playing the role of interpreter was when...
- The consequence or cost of listening to that "wisdom" was...

Secret Service Agent
- An example of my mind playing the role of secret service agent was when...
- The consequence or cost of listening to that "wisdom" was...

Psychologist
- An example of my mind playing the role of psychologist was when...
- The consequence or cost of listening to that "wisdom" was...

Psychic
- An example of my mind playing the role of psychic was when...
- The consequence or cost of listening to that "wisdom" was...

— 5 —

MIND

&

Presence

"Do you have the patience to wait 'till your mud settles and the water is clear? Can you remain unmoving 'till the right action arises by itself?"
~ Tao Te Ching

I. Am. Scared.

That's sort of a weird thing to say (or write), but it's nevertheless, true. And I'm not necessarily scared of any particular situation or possibility, though at times I am; no, the kind of fear I'm talking about is more structural in nature than circumstantial. It's an undefined sense of feeling *separate*, a background feeling of being fundamentally alone and left to fend for myself. That's how life often feels to me and it's felt that way for as long as I can remember.

However, unless you're extremely intuitive and perceptive, you wouldn't see it by looking at me. I'm pretty good at hiding it, even from myself. But it's there, like the background hum of a refrigerator, it's always there. And because I feel separate and alone, I live with a subtle sense of *threat*. It's a vague feeling of being vulnerable. I have to protect myself. I have to make my own way and I have to figure out how to get my needs met. That's the stage on which my life plays out.

In response to this, my mind takes on roles like the ones we discussed in the last chapter. It simply has to. My mind will do whatever it takes to make me feel connected and safe, for that's its job.

"The job of the mind is to guarantee the survival of the being."
~ Brad Blanton [32]

Therefore, my mind becomes my *matchmaker* because it believes that finding me a partner will fix that feeling of being separate. And it becomes my *interpreter, secret service agent, psychologist* and *psychic* in an effort to figure everything out and protect me from harm.

Can you relate to any of this? I bet you can. I realize that we don't openly talk about these kinds of things, we instead medicate these feelings by drinking, getting high or taking meds like *Prozac* and *Xanax*. But our lives will never change if we don't start getting real. So, perhaps you'd use different words, but I think that you're brave enough to admit that even though you may be surrounded by friends and family, as I am, at the core of your personality, there exists a terrifying sense of being alone and left to fend for yourself.

"The mass of men live lives of quiet desperation."
~ Henry David Thoreau

---

[32] *Practicing Radical Honesty,* by Brad Blanton

And as a result, your Personal Mind, like mine, creates all these roles and personas we've been discussing in an attempt to cope with this fundamental feeling of being separate and alone.

PERSONAL MIND

Now, as we saw in the last chapter, our Personal Minds are an untrustworthy source of wisdom and guidance, partly because its perspective is limited and incomplete, but even more so because of what I've just described! The Personal Mind is terrified. It sees everything through the lens of fear, and so its advice is warped and distorted as a result.

Why do you think we use affirmations and practice positive thinking? It's because the mind is so negative, paranoid and neurotic. It takes everything personally, it gets triggered by the stupidest things, it makes up crazy stories and it always assumes the worst.

Listening to your Personal Mind is like getting life coaching from a lunatic.

But it gets worse.

Besides the mind's limited information and its fear-based perspective, it's also chock-full of toxic emotional residue from the past.[33] The mind's favorite hobby is collecting bad experiences, and so the content of our thinking—what that "voice in the head" actually talks about—comes from the bad experiences we've not allowed to pass through us. *In other words, the mind is like a landfill. It's where we store our emotional garbage, and our moment-to-moment thoughts are like the odor rising off of that pile of garbage!* So, when our mind talks, it's literally the garbage that's gabbing, and we'd be nuts to listen to that.

---

[33] The Yogic (Hindu) tradition calls this "Samskaras," Eckhart Tolle calls it the "Pain-Body," and popular culture calls it "baggage." Different names for the same thing.

So, now we have three reasons to not listen to our Personal Minds:

1. Its wisdom is limited and incomplete. It doesn't know anything.
2. Its perspective is fear-based. It's a neurotic mess.
3. It's literally full of shit. The garbage is gabbing.

No wonder Michael Singer says, "I'd rather listen to a Magic 8-Ball than listen to my own mind." He's exactly right. But if those three reasons don't convince you to not listen to "the voice in the head"—and perhaps even to laugh at it—if the idea of not paying attention to your own thinking still seems too radical and outrageous to truly consider, did you know that it's also taught in the Bible (and in pretty much every ancient spiritual text)? There are many verses that speak about the danger of listening to the Personal Mind,[34] but Proverbs 3:5-6 probably says it best:

> "Trust in the Lord with all your heart, *and do not lean on your own understanding.* In all your ways acknowledge Him, and He will make your paths straight."

Do not lean on your own understanding. Could it be any clearer than that? I think the writer of this proverb understood the nature of the mind and how untrustworthy it is. But then that leaves us right where we were at the end of the last chapter. If we don't listen to our own minds, how do we make decisions about "life, love and the pursuit of intimacy?"

PRESENCE MIND

Well, the answer is we don't. We don't have to make decisions, they will be made for us. We don't have to figure everything out, things will work themselves out. We don't have to control things, things are already under

---

[34] Genesis 2:17; Ephesians 4:22-24; 2 Corinthians 10:5, to name a few.

control. And we certainly don't need our minds to play any of the roles we've been discussing. Instead, we can simply relax in PRESENCE and TRUST.

Presence is the state of being that emerges when, as the Tao says, *"the mud settles and the water is clear."* In other words, Presence is when you're not feeling triggered, threatened or reactive. It's when you're not all stirred up on the inside, trying to figure everything out and control everything. *Presence is inner stillness.*

Trust is the attitude or behavior of Presence. It's *knowing*, deep in your bones, that you are and will be OK no matter what happens. Trust is experienced as an unquestioned sense of safety and security that does not come from circumstances, but from a deep confidence that the universe is fundamentally good and trustworthy.

When "the mud settles" and we can trust like this, it dramatically changes how we live. In those moments when we feel confused, anxious or vulnerable, instead of trying to figure it all out and control everything, we can shift from fear to trust, and know that no matter what happens, we are and will be OK. Trust allows us to breathe, open our hearts and let go. It gives Life the space to unfold without us having to DO anything. Trust invites us to relax our grip, to wait and let things play out, and allow an action or a response to arise all by itself.[35]

In Presence, you give Life the space to answer your questions, to make your decisions, and to "make your paths straight."

What I'm suggesting is that you stop interfering with Life, and instead, relax in Presence and allow things to be revealed in their own time. Instead of going up into your head and listening to all of its garbage, and then taking

---

[35] Trust will be explored on a much deeper level when we get to Section Four: *Strengthening Your Relationship to Your Past.*

matters into your own hands (and usually making things worse), what if you took your hands off the wheel and let Life drive?

What would happen?

Well, that would depend on how you see the universe (or God), wouldn't it? If it's a cold, cruel world, then you'd feel alone and left to fend for yourself. But what if, as Einstein wondered, the world is beyond benign to the point of actually being benevolent? What if Life is actually *for us?*

In *Facets of Unity*, A.H. Almaas wrote this:

> "Basic Trust is a non-conceptual, implicit trust or confidence that what is optimal will happen, the sense that no matter what happens, all is well and will be well. It is the confidence that reality is ultimately good; that nature, the universe, and all that exists is "for you," that its very nature is trustworthy."[36]

He's basically channeling what King David wrote thousands of years ago in Psalm 23:

> "The Lord is my shepherd; I shall not want. He makes me lie down in green pastures; He leads me beside quiet waters…Even though I walk through the valley of the shadow of death, I fear no evil; for Thou are with me…Surely goodness and lovingkindness will follow me all the days of my life."[37]

So, how do you see the universe? Are you separate and alone, left to fend for yourself, or is "the universe, and all that exists, *for you"?* Which is it? Are you on your own, or is the Lord your shepherd? Well, if you're like me, it's both. When I listen to the Personal Mind and it tells me that I'm alone and that I have to figure things out, I become an emotional mess. But when

---

[36] A.H. Almaas writes beautifully on the topic of what he calls "Basic Trust" and many of his ideas are expressed in this chapter.
[37] This is not the entire Psalm, just pieces of it.

I'm in Presence Mind, I'm relaxed and trusting that I'm not the doer, but that I'm being done.

PERSONAL MIND vs PRESENCE MIND

Let's get practical. Here are some examples of relationship situations where the Personal Mind and Presence Mind will have very different perspectives. Let's eavesdrop on these two minds.

Scenario #1—A long-distance relationship: You met online about a month ago. You've seen each other once and it's going really well.

Personal Mind:

"I'm getting nervous. Where is this going and how is it going to work? If things continue to progress, do I move or do they? But I don't want to move. I love my job and all my friends are here. Oh, God. Am I wasting my time? I better start talking about our future. I know we've only seen each other once, but still, I need to figure out what they're thinking and where this is going so that I don't end up getting hurt."

Presence Mind:

"Relax! Get out of your head and allow the relationship to go where it wants. You do not have to answer any of these questions. Give the relationship space and the questions will be answered all by themselves."

Scenario #2—A new relationship: Your first date was spectacular, and the chemistry is off the charts. You're seeing them again soon and you're wondering about sex.

Personal Mind:

"God, I want them so much! But it's too soon, right? They'll think I do this with everyone. And what if they're a player and I never see them again? I could get hurt. Should we talk about being exclusive first? But what if they kiss me and it buckles my knees? What do I do then? I need a plan. And what about our profiles? Should I insist we take them down? Is that moving too fast, though? I wonder if they're thinking about this? Probably not. I have to figure this out. I need to find out what they want and if they're interested in anything more than just sex."

Presence Mind:

"Just go enjoy the damn date and quit listening to all that nonsense! Let the relationship unfold. You don't need a plan. Just go be with the person. Open your heart and if the momentum of your relationship is moving toward sex, trust that if there needs to be a conversation about exclusivity or your profiles (and it might not be necessary, it might be obvious), it will occur all by itself, without you obsessing about it and forcing it."

Scenario #3—Dating a newly divorced person: You've been seeing someone for two months and you're the first person they've had any serious feelings for since their divorce became final.

Personal Mind:

"You better be careful. You need to figure out if you're their "rebound relationship." Don't tell them you're scared about this, however. Don't talk with them. They might think you're insecure or something. So just ask a lot of questions and pay really close attention to how they talk about their ex. Find out if they're seeing a therapist too, because if they are, you know what that means! And definitely keep your options open. Even though you really like them, and they seem grounded, you can't go "all in" before you know that they aren't going to wake up one day and realize they aren't ready for another relationship."

Presence Mind:

"Out your feelings immediately! Tell them exactly what that "voice in the head" is saying. And don't pull away by keeping your options open if you're doing that because you're scared. Be present and trust. This relationship may or may not "go the distance"—there's never a guarantee of that with anyone—but the two of you are together for a purpose, so be curious about what that is. Enjoy them, open your heart and trust that no matter how things turn out, it will be for your learning and growth."

In the end, we have to choose—moment by moment—if we're going to pay attention to the stirred up Personal Mind or if we're going to relax in the stillness of Presence and give Life the space to answer our questions, make our decisions and direct our paths. So, I want to end this chapter the same way I started it:

"Do you have the patience to wait till your mud settles and the water is clear?
Can you remain unmoving till the right action arises by itself?"
~ Tao Te Ching [38]

WORKOUT!

Here's a 3-part "workout" to help you practice this in your own life:

1. In your journal, describe three different scenarios that have you stirred up. They do not all have to be intimate relationship issues, either. They can be scenarios happening at work or with a friend. Anything that's got you stirred up will do.

2. For each scenario, write down what the Personal Mind says about it and what Presence Mind says about it. (In other words, do what I did above.)

3. Finally, for each scenario, ask yourself this question and be as honest as possible:

Are you willing to ignore the Personal Mind and its "wisdom," and choose instead to embody the attitude and behavior that comes from Presence Mind?

---

[38] *Tao Te Ching, A New English Version,* by Stephen Mitchell. This is one of the oldest and best spiritual texts ever written and it's pronounced "dow-day-ching".

— 6 —

MIND

&

The Law of Attraction

"The law of attraction is real and that should scare the hell out of you."
~ Michael Singer

I am about to commit heresy. In fact, I could be accused of outright relationship blasphemy. I'm going to dare to challenge what is perhaps the most popular relationship perspective in the world today, the *Law of Attraction*. I'm going to show you why using it is the absolute worst thing you can do for your love life.

I realize I'm going against conventional wisdom and slaughtering a sacred cow of sorts. Nearly every relationship expert on earth says the *Law of Attraction* (LOA) is the key to finding your ideal partner, and for years that included me.[39] But as I've continued to evolve and grow in my understanding of both the human condition and intimate relationships, I now see that using the LOA will ruin your love life and sabotage your ability to experience authentic intimacy.

A little background might help. The LOA first appeared, as far as I can tell, in the late 1800's, and while it gained traction because of books like Napoleon Hill's *Think and Grow Rich* (1937) and Normal Vincent Peale's,

---

[39] In some of my eCourses and books (created before 2014), I advised people to create a list of qualities they want in a partner. As this chapter will show, I now think that's not only unnecessary, but it's actually counterproductive.

The Power of Positive Thinking (1952), it didn't explode in popularity until Oprah Winfrey fully endorsed Ronda Byrne's movie, *The Secret* in 2006. Since then, it's become THE dominant teaching on how to find your life partner.

WHAT IS THE LAW OF ATTRACTION?

I'm sure you already know this, but the basic teaching of the LOA, as it pertains to relationships anyway, is to have a clear idea or vision of "the one" you want to attract, your ideal partner. The thinking is, how can the universe (or God) bring you your ideal partner if you don't describe who that person is? It's like going to a restaurant. How can the server bring you something if you don't tell them what you want? So, we're told to make a list of qualities we want and don't want in a partner. Sometimes this list is called our "absolute yeses and noes," or our "must-haves and can't stands." Other times we create a vision board or visualize during meditation or even write in our prayer journals. No matter how we express our wants, according to the LOA, if we want to attract "The One" we must first describe "The One."

OK, fair enough. I'm not questioning the basic idea that in order to manifest something we first have to define or visualize it. That's true on a certain level. Nor am I taking issue with the LOA because it doesn't work. It most certainly does![40] But that's the problem. *My issue with the LOA is why we use it in the first place.* To explain, I need to refresh your memory.

MATCHMAKER

Back in Chapter 2, I said that we all have some sort of "not OK" feeling on the inside. Perhaps it's feeling undesirable, lonely or not good enough. No

---

[40] Esther Hicks, and other false teachers like her, actually teach that your thoughts can create a reality. It's funny, though. They don't have an answer as to why they or their followers don't win the lottery every week. So, when I say the LOA works, I don't mean it works like *THAT*. If you're interested in how these types of insane LOA teachings have been thoroughly debunked, a good place to start is by reading Dr. Neil Farber's article in Psychology Today: https://bit.ly/2zZTHFE

matter what it is, it's so intolerable that we seek a relationship to fix it, and that requires a certain kind of person–someone qualified for the job, you could say. Enter the Personal Mind as *matchmaker*. Its role is to define who that "ideal partner" needs to be and then help you find them. Our list, therefore, describes the kind of partner we need to fix our "not OK" feeling (or at least not trigger it).

Here are three examples, the first of which is from my life:

1. My particular "not OK" feeling was being undesirable, so guess what quality appeared first on my list? "I want a woman who loves sex." Makes perfect sense, doesn't it? That kind of woman fixes my undesirable issue. And I found her. Near the end of my first marriage, I met "Julie" and for months we had sex like rabbits.[41] I was in heaven. I was finally desirable! But when she began focusing more on her career, our sexual activity slowed down and that triggered my undesirable feeling again. So, I started pressuring her for sex and soon she dumped me.

2. Let's say your particular "not OK" feeling was loneliness. In that case, your list would say, "my ideal partner needs to be emotionally available," or something to that effect. You will look for a person who's willing and able to make you the center of their attention. That way you'll never feel lonely. But if they start spending more time at work or with their friends, or if they find a new hobby or interest, you'll feel lonely again and you'll pressure them to re-prioritize you, and the relationship will begin to die a slow (or maybe a quick) death.

---

[41] "Julie" is the main character in my first book, *A Drink with Legs*, but it's not her real name.

3. If someone's issue is insecurity, their list would say something like, "my partner must be loyal and trustworthy." But the minute they so much as look at another person, or God forbid, flirt with someone! or if they don't respond to your texts or voice mails quickly enough, that insecure feeling will resurface, and you'll become angry and controlling, demanding that they get back in line. Their job is to keep you from feeling insecure and they better get back to work! That relationship, too, is on its way to ending.

Those are three examples of the LOA at work and it's not a very pretty picture, is it? The reason why we use LOA is to find our *ideal* partner, someone who's uniquely qualified to fix our particular "not OK" feeling. This means we're expecting our life partner to be our Life Source, that we've bought into the "you complete me" mindset. As a result, we have just ruined our love life.

Furthermore—and this is where it gets really frightening—because "like attracts like," which is what the LOA actually means, *you'll attract someone who wants you to fix their "not OK" feeling too.* In other words, they'll see you as their Life Source, too! So, an unconscious deal of sorts is struck: Your job is to fix my "not OK" feeling, and my job is to fix yours. This is co-dependence and it's what the Law of Attraction creates.

The Law of Attraction is nothing more than co-dependence dressed up in drag.

Co-dependence is an unconscious agreement to fix one another. Both people are depending on the other to be their Life Source, and it might work for a while, as it did for me and Julie, but eventually it will end in disaster because life partners make lousy Life Sources.

Now are you seeing why the LOA should scare the hell out of you? It doesn't attract love, it attracts co-dependence!

Using the Law of Attraction as your strategy for finding an intimate partner is like using bank robbery as your strategy for making money. Yes, you'll make some money, but you'll ruin your life in the process.

BREAK THE LAW

If you want any chance at a healthy, sustainable relationship, you have to get rid of your list and, especially, the mindset that created it. However, this brings us back to the dilemma we faced earlier. If we don't ask the Personal Mind to be our matchmaker, how in the world are we supposed to find a partner or choose the right person? Well, as you might expect, there is a much better way—*and spoiler alert!*—it has something to do with "arranged marriages."

But before I explain that, it's paramount that you completely abandon the Law of Attraction mindset because you won't be open to any other approach unless you're convinced it will ruin your love life. So, besides creating co-dependence, here are 7 more reasons to break the Law.

1. Mystics are Morons

The Law of Attraction is about manifesting what you want, right? Whether it's a house, a job or a relationship, the LOA is about how to get what you want. But wait a minute. Buddhism's most basic teaching is that the root of suffering is *wanting*. So, what gives? The LOA says wanting is good, Buddhism says the opposite. Which is it?

What's weird is that most of the people who teach the LOA are very pro-Buddhism, yet they don't seem to see the inherent contradiction! The LOA is completely at odds with Buddhism. The two are like oil and water.

But the same goes for Christianity. The Bible doesn't promote wanting. Here are a couple of examples:

- *"What will it profit a man if he gains the whole world and yet forfeits his soul?"*
- *"Do not store up for yourselves treasures on earth…"*
- *"The love of money is a root of all sorts of evil."*[42]

Buddha and Jesus are probably the most profound spiritual teachers that have ever walked the face of the earth. No one has taught more powerfully on how to be happy and lead a meaningful life than they have. So, if I'm asked to choose between Buddha and Jesus, whose wisdom has stood the test of time, and the LOA, I'm going "old school." Yet, if you listen to those who teach the LOA, it's as if they think these two mystics were morons.

"There is nothing spiritual about the Law of Attraction."
~ Michael Singer

---

2. "I Want Ice Cream!"

By making a list that describes what we want in a partner, we're telling the universe (or God) that we know what's best for us, and I have serious doubts that we do. Imagine a 3-year old telling its parents that a steady diet of ice cream is exactly what they need to grow! That's nuts, right? But that's essentially what we're doing with our lists. We think we know what's best for us—*but do we?* There have been many times where I threw a temper

---

[42] Mark 8:36, Matthew 6:19 and 1 Timothy 6:10 respectively.

tantrum at the universe because I didn't get what I wanted, only to later discover that Life knew what was best for me.

Since our lists come from the untrustworthy Personal Mind, wouldn't it be better to scrap it and trust that if or when a relationship would serve our evolution, that Life will put us with the person that's best for us?

3. Mission Impossible

Third, have you taken an objective look at your list lately? Does that person even exist? *"I want someone who has a great career and is financially stable. They must have impeccable character, spiritual depth and a great sense of humor. They need to be physically hot, emotionally available and great in the sack. Oh, and they have to love dogs, children and Jesus!"* Do you see what I mean? Who could measure up to that? Hell, would you qualify to date yourself?

4. A Weird Threesome

Have you thought about how you come up with the things on your list in the first place? It's completely based on your past. **Your list doesn't describe your ideal partner, it describes your emotional baggage!** Every single thing on your list describes something you haven't let go of.

As I mentioned earlier, my ideal partner had to love sex. Why? Because my ex didn't! So, whenever I met someone new, my past stood between us. It was like having a really weird threesome! I was not interacting with them, but with the pain from my past, and then holding them responsible to fix it! Consequently, my relationships never worked out. If you have a list, the best you can hope for is a threesome from hell: you, them and your past.

5. The Law of Impermanence

When I signed yearbooks back in high school, I'd often write, "don't ever change." It's sweet but utterly ridiculous. Everybody changes. One of the problems with making a list is that even if you could find someone who met your criteria (and you can't), they won't continue to meet your criteria for very long. It's the law of impermanence. The qualities they possess today will change because experience constantly alters the psyche and personality. So even if you could find your ideal partner, you can't count on them to stay that way! So why bother with a list at all?

6. Physician, Heal Thyself!

However we would describe our particular "not OK" feeling, if we can't fix that ourselves, what makes us think someone else can? We've addressed this before, but it needs to be repeated. As I heard Michael Singer say one time: *"How can someone on the outside of you fix the inside of you, when you can't fix the inside of you and you live in there 24/7?"*

7. Relational Waterboarding

If we have a list, we will interrogate those we date. It has to be that way. Yes, we'll do our best not to be obvious about it, but we have to find out if they meet our criteria. What's the purpose of having a list if we're not going to find out if they measure up to it? Dating, then, becomes an interview at best, and an interrogation at worst!

Using the LOA will turn you into a relationship waterboard-er: *Who are you! Tell me the truth! Do you want to get married someday? Yes or no! Are you a player? Can I trust you? Tell me! How much money do you make? Do you have any debt? Have you cheated in the past? Don't lie to me! Are you emotionally available? Are you high maintenance? Do you love drama? Are you addicted to anything? Tell me right now!!*

ARRANGED MARRIAGES

Now that I have obliterated the Law of Attraction and hopefully convinced you to abandon that mindset forever, questions like these remain: "If I don't have a list, how am I supposed to choose a partner? Should I have no standards? Should I just go out with anyone?" Obviously not.

Don't overcomplicate this. You will quite naturally find yourself interested in certain people and not in others. It's just how life works. You don't need to think about it or worry about it or force it (and you certainly don't need some ridiculous mind-made list). People meet each other, they like each other, and relationships happen.

Does the flower fret about where and how it will find a bee, or what kind of bee it needs? *"I need a bee with big strong wings and a great big stinger!"* No, the flower doesn't do any of that. In fact, it doesn't DO anything. It just sits there—smelling good and looking pretty. It completely trusts that if Life wants it to be "pollinated," then Life will *arrange* a relationship with the right kind of bee at the right time. *The flower simply rests in Presence and trusts.*

And what about the bee? Is it stressed out about where to find a beautiful flower? Is it at the "bee bar" buzzing with its "bee buddies" about what field to fly over in search of the one single flower it needs to be happy? *"Where will I find a flower with a long, thin stem and big pedals?"* No, the bee just…flies, and it completely trusts that Life will arrange a relationship with just the right flower. There is no mind involved. There are no decisions being made. Life is arranging the whole thing.

Why do we make this so hard? Why do we take responsibility for *arranging* what is actually none of our business? The flowers and bees certainly don't do that…and they end up finding each other just fine.

Why can't we let go and let Life arrange our relationships?

You don't have to find your partner. *You* don't have to figure anything out. *You* don't have to make anything happen. But *you* can let go—completely—and trust. And one day you'll wake up and see a person lying next to you in bed and think, "This is so cool! How did they get here, how did this happen?" Answer? Who the hell knows! How does the bee find the flower? It just happens.

However, one thing I know for sure: You don't need a damn list. You can trust that life is unfolding perfectly, that all is well and will be well. Just as David trusted that the Lord, as his shepherd, would take care of him, leading him to "green pastures and quiet waters," so you can relax and trust that Life will take care of you.

WORKOUT!

Sometimes on late-night talk shows, comedians will do a funny bit where they play an actual sound bite from a politician (or some other public figure), and then translate their words, telling us what they really meant. It can be pretty hilarious.

I'd like you to do that with your list (though it might not be as hilarious). In your journal, take one or two of the most important qualities you want in your partner and translate it. Describe what you're really wanting from your partner. Here are some examples based upon what was discussed earlier in this chapter.

> **Roy's List:** "I want a woman who loves sex."
> **Translation:** "I want a woman who will take responsibility for fixing my undesirable feeling by having sex with me whenever I want."

> **The Lonely Person's List:** "I want a partner who is emotionally available."

Translation: "I want a partner who will take responsibility for fixing my loneliness by always choosing me over work, family, friends or hobbies.

The Insecure Person's List: "I want my partner to be loyal and trustworthy."

Translation: "I want a partner who will take responsibility for fixing my insecurity by never talking to a member of the opposite sex and by responding to my communications immediately.

— 7 —

MIND

&

Monkey Business

"All problems are caused by mind. No exceptions."
~ Michael Singer

When I was a kid, I used to love going to the zoo. The big cats were (and still are) my favorite animals, but second to them were the monkeys. Their exhibit is absolute chaos and it's hilarious to watch. They motor around, swinging on ropes, leaping from tree branch to tree branch, and they even sometimes jump on each other. It's just non-stop action. And the noise is incredible too! Ear-piercing screeching, screaming and cackling. It's utter pandemonium.

Well, you've probably heard the phrase, "The Monkey Mind." I think the Buddhists originally coined it, but anybody who takes even a minute to watch what's happening in their heads can perfectly understand the metaphor. The Personal Mind is like the monkey exhibit at the zoo. It's just chaos. It's is all over the place, jumping randomly from one thought to another. It's never still. And it's really noisy too. That "voice in the head" is always cackling about something. It just never shuts up.

Sam Harris describes it this way:

> "When you sit down to meditate, you meet your mind, and your mind is the most rambling, chaotic, needling, insulting, insufferable person you will ever meet. It's like having some maniac walk through the front door of your house and follow you from room to room and refuse to stop talking. And this happens every day of your life."[43]

In this section of the book, we've been focusing on strengthening your relationship to your mind. And up until now, the discussion has been about *why* you shouldn't listen to it, why the Personal Mind isn't a trustworthy source of wisdom and guidance. We've seen that not only does it have access to very limited information, but it's a fearful, neurotic mess, filled with garbage from the past. Therefore, it's far better to laugh at the mind's "monkey business" than to listen to it. But we haven't said much about *how* to do that. How do we not listen to our own thinking? That seems challenging, and in fact, it is.

So, in the final chapter of this section, I want to give you two life-changing techniques or tools to help you grow stronger in your ability to ignore and laugh at the "monkey mind" rather than listening to it and letting it ruin your life.

Let's get something straight, however. I'm not talking about quieting the mind or shutting it up. That is not possible and it's not the goal.[44] The mind is not like a radio that you can turn off. You can't make it stop jumping from "thought branch" to "thought branch" any more than you could stop the monkeys from jumping around at the zoo. But you can ignore it and stop listening to it, and I realize that's easier said than done. That's why I want to

---

[43] This is a quote from *The Waking Up Course*, which is Harris' mediation App.
[44] I'm told that after *decades* of meditation, the mind does quiet down. I think it was Yogananda, the great Indian spiritual teacher of the 20th century that said, "An ignored guest quickly leaves." But since you probably haven't been meditating for decades, nor have I, we'll take baby steps and start with an attainable goal like ignoring the mind, and perhaps one day that annoying "guest" will leave, meaning, it will shut the hell up.

give you two tools to help you strengthen the relationship you have with your mind.

YOU ARE NOT YOUR MIND

But there's a critical understanding that is needed in order to effectively use the two techniques that follow. This may seem obvious, but it's actually quite profound. *You are not your mind.* You are not the voice that talks in your head, you are the one who hears it. This is where the monkey exhibit metaphor continues to be helpful. At the zoo, you are not the monkeys, you're the one watching them. Believe it or not, recognizing this is the first step to liberation.

Once you realize you are not the Personal Mind but are instead the one who watches it or observes it, you're free to do whatever you want with it.

Here's another way to understand this: Outside my office window is a tree. If I can see the tree, I can't be the tree, right? I'm the one looking at it. Therefore, I can do anything I want with that tree. I can go outside and climb it, or I could get an axe and chop it down. I could hug it, I could "TP" it, or I could ignore it. Since I am not the tree, I can do whatever I want with it.

That's how it is with your mind. It's just like the tree. You can do whatever you want with it. You can listen to what it says and take its advice (to your peril), or you can laugh at what it says and ignore its advice (to your joy). You can do whatever you want because you're not the mind, you're the one listening to it.

With that understanding, here are two techniques for growing stronger in your ability to not listen to the Personal Mind.

PRACTICE #1: MEDITATION—Sam Harris', The Waking Up Course

Let me be as direct as possible. If you don't commit to a regular meditation practice, your love life is never going to be as satisfying as it could be. Believing its stories and listening to its "wisdom" is the cause of every problem in your life, so your mind is literally your worst enemy. Therefore, if you allow the "monkey mind" to run wild, it will ruin your life.

Meditation is practicing not listening to the mind and it's essential that you regularly practice it.

Now, even though meditation is the simplest thing in the world to do—you just sit there and pay attention—for many, it's scary and even intimidating. Most people (including me) need some guidance and structure. And that's where *The Waking Up Course* developed by Sam Harris comes in. (Click the link if you're reading this book digitally, otherwise Google it.)

The Waking Up Course is a 50-day guided meditation program. Each mediation is about 10 minutes long and it's perfect for both the beginner and the experienced meditator. What's cool is that once the 50-day course is completed, the App has new mediations uploaded daily so that you can continue to practice.

This App is not free, however. After about Day 7 you'll be asked to subscribe. If money is an issue, you can use *Headspace* or *Insight Timer*, but I like *The Waking Up Course* much better (it includes teaching lessons from Harris and he's brilliant). As of this writing, a one-year subscription costs $119.99. That's $10 a month and it's well worth the investment.[45]

---

[45] If you send an email to info@wakingup.com and request a free one-year subscription, they will give it to you.

PRACTICE #2: INQUIRY—Byron Katie's, <u>The Work</u>

Meditation is practicing not listening to the mind. It's all about ignoring that "voice in the head." However, sometimes you may find that you can't ignore a thought. Sometimes a thought seems so true that it feels like it's Velcro-ed to your very soul. It's just too sticky, too real and too "true" to ignore. In that case, a more proactive approach is necessary, something that is called, *Inquiry*.

Inquiry is a formal process of putting a sticky, stressful thought on paper and questioning it. It's a process of interrogating any belief, story or assumption that is causing any degree of suffering. And I have found no inquiry method better than Byron Katie's, *The Work*. It's an incredible 4-question process that is designed to help you reframe, and ultimately release, any sort of stressful thought. I am going to suggest that you not only go to her website, but that you live there for about a month! (Again, click the link or Google it.) There are literally dozens of videos on the site of her doing *The Work* with people on a variety of issues.

Here's a little bit of Katie's story. In the mid-80's, in the midst of a ten-year-long depression she had a life-changing realization that she described this way:

> "I discovered that when I believed my thoughts, I suffered, but that when I didn't believe them, I didn't suffer, and that this is true for every human being. Freedom is as simple as that. I found that suffering is optional. I found a joy within me that has never disappeared, not for a single moment. That joy is in everyone, always."

From that experience, she created *The Work*, a simple 4-question process to help herself and others examine the beliefs that cause suffering. The four questions are:

1. *Is it true?*

2. *Can you absolutely know that it's true?*

3. *How do you react, what happens, when you believe that thought?*

4. *Who would you be without the thought?*

The follow-up step to these four questions is something she calls "the turnaround." This allows us to experience that the opposite of our story or belief is at least as true, if not truer than, our original thought."[46]

WORKOUT!

Your "workout," then, is twofold. First, download *The Waking Up Course App* and use it to meditate every day (or do some other type of meditation). Secondly, study and use Byron Katie's, *The Work* as if your life depended on it, because it does.

---

[46] You'll remember we talked about this in Chapter 4.

WORKOUT #3

STRENGTHENING YOUR RELATIONSHIP TO YOUR FEELINGS

AVOID or FEEL

"Much evidence testifies that people who are emotionally adept—who know and manage their own feelings well, and who read and deal effectively with other people's feelings—are at an advantage in any domain of life, whether romance or intimate relationships or picking up the unspoken rules that govern success in organizational politics."
~ Daniel Goleman

— 8 —

FEELINGS

&

Being Emotionally Smarter Than a 5th Grader

"In the last decade or so, science has discovered a tremendous amount about the role emotions play in our lives. Researchers have found that even more than IQ, your emotional awareness and abilities to handle feelings will determine your success and happiness in all walks of life, including intimate relationships."

~ John Gottman [47]

In most professions, there's a particular kind of ability or talent that is needed in order to be successful. For example, a therapist needs to be a good listener, a baseball pitcher needs a strong, accurate arm and an accountant needs to be good with numbers. If a person doesn't have the necessary ability for their profession—or if they don't have enough of it—they will struggle to be successful.

The same is true in relationships. In order to be relationally successful, we need a particular kind of talent or ability and that's something called *Emotional Intelligence* (EQ). It is arguably the single most important skill needed to have a successful love life. In fact, as the above quotes indicate, researchers are finding that EQ is the "secret sauce" to almost everything.

---

[47] Gottman is perhaps the most famous couples' therapist and relationship researcher in the world today. I found this quote on the Internet and although I know he said it, I don't know where it came from.

It's now understood that even if we have an IQ that is off the charts or even if we have the highest levels of athletic or artistic ability, if we don't have EQ—if we don't know how to deal with our feelings and the feelings of others—we are at a disadvantage in just about every aspect of life. For example, with low Emotional Intelligence...

- Professionally, our career paths may stagnate and not progress as they should.
- Socially, we'll end up with acquaintances rather than deeply connected friendships.
- Parentally, we'll wound our children and make it difficult for them to bond with others later in life.
- Spiritually, we'll stunt our own growth by disconnecting from the emotional wisdom found in our bodies.
- Intimately, we'll experience constant drama and probably end up dumped, divorced and alone.

It would be nearly impossible to overstate the importance of EQ. Life is a contact sport, and we are not in contact with machines, we're in contact with hearts—ours and others. And if we're not skillful in matters of the heart, our love lives will suffer, as will all aspects of our lives.

Fortunately, in order to have a great love life, we don't need to be Einstein-like geniuses when it comes to Emotional Intelligence. We don't need a master's degree or even an undergraduate degree.

All that's necessary to be successful in our pursuit of intimacy is to be emotionally smarter than a 5th grader.

THE "K.I.S.S." APPROACH

In this section, as we focus on strengthening our relationship to our feelings, we're going to use the "K.I.S.S." approach (*Keep It Simple Stupid*) as much as possible. EQ is a very complex issue and we've had virtually no training or education in it. When it comes to feelings and matters of the heart, it's often an area of life where we are either uneducated or undereducated or miseducated (take your pick).

For example, in school, we all learned to read and write. We also learned math, science, history and perhaps even a second language. But did you have a class on feelings? Did you spend a quarter or a semester learning how to express anger, fear or sadness in a way that restored a sense of inner peace and created harmony with others?

How about in your place of worship? Did you ever hear a sermon on how to locate and welcome a feeling in your body and how to feel it all the way through to completion? And how about in your family of origin? Did you sit around the kitchen table and talk about the wisdom of your feelings and what they were here to teach you? I didn't and I doubt you did either.

Emotions and matters of the heart, while critical to our happiness and our ability to connect with others, is an area where we've mostly been left to figure it out on our own. And judging from the toxic world in which we're living, we haven't done a very good job of it. Seems most of our emotional education has either come from the dysfunctional dynamics in our families, or perhaps, from public figures, social media or reality TV (God help us all).

We really are not smarter than a 5th grader when it comes to the emotional realm of life, so I'm going to do my best to uncomplicate a very complicated issue.

FEEL OR AVOID?

If you learn only one thing from this section of the book, I would want it to be this: You can either *FEEL* your feelings, or you can *AVOID* them. Those are the only two choices you have, and EQ is really nothing more than that.

An emotionally intelligent person is one who chooses to FEEL their feelings rather than AVOID them.

Simple, right? Hardly. This "workout" may be the most difficult of all, for it truly is easier said than done. But make no mistake about it, the choice you make, moment-to-moment, to either feel your feelings or avoid them, determines the quality of your entire life and certainly the depth (and duration!) of your relationships.

EQ BASICS

Now, before we dive in and fully explore what it means to feel rather than avoid our feelings, it's important that we understand some basics. And for clarity, I'll present them in a Q & A format.

What is an emotion?[48]

Jim Dethmer defines emotion like this: "Emotion is 'e-motion.' Energy in motion. At its simplest level, emotion is energy moving in or on the body. Or, said another way, feelings are physical sensations."

---

[48] I have learned many of the ideas presented in this section of the book from both Jim Dethmer, co-founder of *The Conscious Leadership Group* and Gay & Kathlyn Hendricks, founders of *The Hendricks Institute.*

Are there good emotions and bad emotions?

No. They, of course, may be handled in destructive or constructive ways (as we'll discuss), but any emotion—even anger—is neither good nor bad, right nor wrong—it just is.

Where do emotions come from?

Emotions arise in response to three different kinds of stimuli:

(1) Emotions occur in response to experience. Life unfolds in front of us, it comes in through our senses and it either *touches* or *triggers* us in a way that stimulates a spontaneous, thoughtless reaction, i.e., an emotion.

Some examples of being *touched* by an experience are things like being approached by an extremely attractive person at a party, walking in the woods and coming upon a bear or seeing an adorable little puppy. Those experiences would spontaneously produce sexual feelings, fear and joy, respectively.

But sometimes, we're *triggered* by an experience, not merely touched by it. For example, if we see a former partner with someone new or if we're criticized in the same way our mother criticized us, those types of experiences can trigger some sort of old pain or trauma that we've stored in our bodies, and an intense wave of anger, fear or sadness might spontaneously arise.[49]

Whether we're touched or triggered, it doesn't matter. Feelings spontaneously arise in response to experience. And while these kinds of feelings can be extremely intense, they have

---

[49] We touched on this in Chapter 5, and we will go more deeply into the pain stored in our bodies in Chapter 15.

a very short life span. They arise out of nowhere and dissolve almost as quickly, usually in less than 90 seconds—unless we intentionally hold on to them, which we very often do.[50]

(2) Emotions occur in response to our thoughts. For example, if you have the thought that your company might down-size, costing you your job, you can bet an emotion will appear in the body. If you believe that you'll never meet someone special and that you're going to die alone, again, emotions like fear, sadness or even anger will arise in the body. It's guaranteed.

If you look very closely, you'll see that almost all of the really sticky, heavy emotions—the ones that seem to grab us by the throat and won't let go—those emotions are caused by thoughts.

In these situations, emotions do *not* just spontaneously occur. We *create* them by listening to that neurotic, story-telling voice in our heads. Therefore, thought-generated emotions are better understood as MOODS. And the signature difference between an experience-generated *emotion* and a thought-generated *mood* is how long it lasts.

Emotions have a very short life span, while moods last as long as the thought that created it is believed to be true.

In other words, emotions last mere seconds; moods can last decades—if the thoughts that create them are not questioned. Consequently, the way you handle an experience-generated emotion is very different from the way you handle a thought-

---

[50] The research concerning the short life span of emotions is found in, *My Stroke of Genius*, by Jill Bolte-Taylor, a Harvard-trained neuroanatomist.

generated mood, and we'll discuss that in the remaining chapters of this section.

(3) *Emotions occur in response to our desires.* Why does a two-year-old throw a temper tantrum? Answer: because they aren't getting what they want. The same is true of us. As Michael Singer has insightfully said:

> "You don't have to tell me what you're anxious about, depressed about, insecure about or afraid of. I already know. You're worried that you won't get what you want or that you will get what you don't want. You've defined how life needs to be in order for you to be ok, and Life won't cooperate—and it's not supposed to, and it never will. The root of all your emotional distress is as simple as that."

The more you grow in self-awareness, the more you'll see how true that is. We cause our own suffering. **We make ourselves an emotional wreck by wanting life (people, circumstances, conditions) to be different than it is.** But as we said in Chapter 1, the moment you don't mind what's happening is the moment when emotional turbulence dissolves and peace fills the soul.[51]

Don't other people cause my emotions?

No, but I'll admit it certainly looks that way. But if you look closely, you'll see that people don't have the power to make us feel any particular way: happy or hurt, angry or aroused, scared or serene. We're the only ones

---

[51] All of Section 1 was devoted to this subject, so I won't be touching on it here in this section. I'll only deal with the first two sources of emotional upset: experience-generated feelings and thought-generated feelings.

that live inside, and no one has the ability to control our inner experience—unless we let them.

For example (and perhaps you can relate to this), I often get really angry at people who drive slowly. Are they *making* me angry? No. They're just doing what they're doing. I'm choosing to get angry because I've decided how they are supposed to drive, and they aren't cooperating.

That's true in every situation, no matter what it is. Even though we frequently say things like, *"You make me so angry!"* or *"You hurt my feelings!"*, while it might be understandable that we feel angry or hurt, in reality, those statements are not true. We've made ourselves angry and we've hurt our own feelings by believing that people should behave the way we want them to.

What are the primary emotions?

Well, just as red, blue and yellow are primary colors, and every other color is a combination of those three, so there are five primary emotions and all other emotions are a combination of them.

The five primary emotions are: Angry, sad, scared, joyful and sexual feelings.[52] While there are literally hundreds of words in the English language that describe different emotional states, you'll find that they all fall into one of these five categories. And each category has a spectrum of intensity, from low to high.

For example, words like "annoyed" or "irritated" might be used to describe low-intensity anger, while words like "furious" or "enraged" describe higher intensity anger. Either way, they all fall into the angry category and all five primary emotions can be thought of this way.

---

[52] In Daniel Goleman's ground-breaking book, *Emotional Intelligence*, he lists "love" as a primary feeling. I disagree, as do most spiritual teachers. Feelings come and go based on conditions (experiences, thoughts & desires), while love (if it's actually love and not lust) is unconditional. Love is a commitment, not a feeling. By the way, all of Goleman's quotes are from his book, *Emotional Intelligence*.

Also, just as purple is a combination of red and blue, some emotions are a combination of the primary emotions. "Hurt," for example, is a combination of anger and sadness. "Loneliness" is a combination of sad and scared, and "jealous" is a combination of angry, scared and sexual feelings.

Here's a key point:

An emotionally intelligent person drills down to the very core of their experience and speaks the raw, real truth about what they feel.

They don't say, "I feel annoyed," they say, "I feel angry." They don't say, "I feel a little down today," they say, "I feel sad." Something magical happens when we strip away all the self-protective euphemisms and just blurt the raw, real truth.[53]

I like some feelings more than others. Do I have to be open to all five of them?

No, if you don't want to be fully human. I understand that feeling joyful is preferable to feeling sad, but you can't control how life unfolds. And as far as scientists can tell, the earth is the only planet in the universe that has life—and you get to be a part of it!

Water falls out of the sky on your head. That doesn't happen anywhere else in the universe. You get to see majestic mountains and breath-taking sunsets. You can hear music, play with animals, and talk to people! How cool is that? And you want to limit your experience? Are you kidding? You've got 80 or so years on this amazing planet, why wouldn't you want to experience everything it has to offer, both the agony and the ecstasy?

And besides, all the emotions come from the same place inside of us. So, if you avoid or repress one emotion it influences the flow of all the others.

---

[53] More about this when we get to Section 5: *Strengthening Your Relationship to Your Inner Truth.*

Here's how Jim Dethmer puts it in, *The 15 Commitments of Conscious Leadership:*

> "The five emotions flow through the body like water does through a hose. If you kink the hose, the water stops flowing or slows to a trickle. Similarly, if you kink your emotional "hose" (repress emotion), all emotions are affected. Many people would like to block anger but still feel joy, or they'd like to limit sadness but still have sexual feelings. This is very difficult to do."

Sometimes I'm not sure what I'm feeling. Is there a way to tell?

Absolutely, and this is a much bigger problem than you might imagine. It's not unusual for boys (e.g., me) to grow up in an environment where anger is allowed, but feelings like sadness or fear are met with shame and derision. Those boys are told, *"don't be such a pussy,"* or *"big boys don't cry."*

When masculinity is misunderstood like this, boys grow up unable to feel scared or sad. The only feeling that they have access to, then, is anger, and every emotion comes out as that. Therefore, when a man is angry, there's a good chance he's actually scared or perhaps sad, but he doesn't know it. He can't feel his true feelings because he's been forced to disown them.

Young girls can have a similar experience. They often grow up in environments where it's OK to be sad, for example, but it's not OK to be angry. Young girls might hear things like, *"Anger is not lady-like. Girls are supposed to be sensitive, sweet and soft-spoken,"* and when they get older, it might become, *"Calm down! Go to your room and don't come out until you stop being such a bitch!"*

When femininity is misunderstood like this, girls grow up unable to feel the anger that's in their bodies. The only thing they have access to, then, is sadness, and every emotion comes out as that. Therefore, when a woman is crying, there's a good chance she's actually angry, but she doesn't know it. (I've had many women tell me how angry they are with tears streaming down their face.) She truly can't feel her true feelings because she's been forced to disown them.

All of this is to say that we often don't know what we're feeling. But if we want any chance at an authentic relationship, we have to know our authentic feelings and be able to express them in honest, healthy ways.

So, how do we identify our true feelings? By going into the body.

If you go up into your head and think about your feelings, you'll hear all of those crappy messages from your childhood. In other words, your body is not as messed up as your head is. Remember, emotions are nothing more than physical sensations, or energy, moving in the body. So, a person with a high EQ lets their bodily sensations tell them what they are feeling, and not the garbage that's in their heads.

Amazingly, all five of the primary feelings show up in very specific areas of the body. Once you know what region holds which emotion, you can reliably know what you're truly feeling. Here's where each primary emotion is felt in the body:

- **Anger** shows up in the back, shoulders, neck, jaw and hands. That's why we angrily say, "You're such a pain in the neck!"
- **Sadness** shows up in the heart area, as well as the throat and eyes, which is why we say, "I have a broken heart," or "I'm all choked up."
- **Fear** shows up in the belly and solar plexus, which is why we say, "I've got butterflies in my stomach."
- **Joy** is a little different. Normally it's felt throughout the body as an upward surge of energy, which is why we jump to our feet and throw our hands up when our favorite team scores, but sometimes it's

experienced as a calm, content "ahhh" feeling deep in the belly, similar to how you might feel after a great meal.

- **Sexual Feelings** show up in the erogenous zones: the mouth, genitals, hips and pelvis, which is why the sexiest dances (e.g., salsa) are all about the hips.[54]

WORKOUT!

Those are the basics when it comes to EQ. But before we move on and explore the many ways we avoid our feelings, here is a short "workout" assignment.

1. In your journal, choose the primary emotion that you have either disowned or are the least comfortable experiencing and/or expressing.
2. What caused you to have issues with that feeling? What happened? Can you recall a specific time or event where it all started?
3. If you were to express that emotion in your life right now, what do you fear would happen?

---

[54] For example, see: https://bit.ly/1AiAl8y. If this doesn't stir your sexual feelings, I don't know what will. Wow. Notice it's all about the hips.

— 9 —

FEELINGS

&

How to Have A Horrible Life

"All man's miseries derive from not being able to sit quietly in a room alone."

~ Blaise Pascal

Now that we've learned the basics of Emotional Intelligence (EQ), we can address the real issue, which is the choice to either feel or avoid our feelings. And if you're on any sort of spiritual path—Christian, Buddhist, Jewish, Muslim, "spiritual but not religious,"—hell, even if you're an atheist—you know that the conventional wisdom is that it's far better to feel your feelings than it is to avoid them.

But is that true? Should we just take that at face value and not question it? I mean, why should we feel our feelings and not avoid them, especially the uncomfortable ones? Seriously. Why would we purposely move toward a painful emotion and not run away from it? Where's the value in that? It doesn't make sense—unless you want to be a masochist! *If we feel sad, stressed, bored or lonely, for example, why in the world would we want to feel that and not avoid it?* I think that's a legitimate question and one that deserves an answer.

THE EMOTIONAL PARADOX

Let's admit, first of all, that we all want to feel good. Pleasure is preferable to pain. The desire to feel good is a very normal and natural human instinct and there's absolutely nothing wrong with it. In fact, the more you want to feel good, the more you'll be willing to move toward your uncomfortable feelings, not away from them. There's a strange paradox here:

By avoiding our feelings, we actually end up feeling worse, not better.

When we avoid our feelings—and I'm going to show 10 different ways we do that—they don't just go away. *Repressing them doesn't release them.* It sort of pisses them off. There's a scene in *Die Hard*, one of my all-time favorite movies, where John McClane (the hero) is being ignored by Hans Gruber (the villain). John doesn't like that, so he straps a bunch of C-4 to a chair and throws it down an elevator shaft, blowing up the building.[55] That's sort of what happens when we ignore our feelings. They take revenge on us, doing incredible damage to our lives—relationally, physically, energetically and behaviorally.

For example, when an emotion like anger is suppressed, it damages our relationships because it eventually explodes, usually all over our partners. And avoiding our feelings damages us physically too. Stress damages the heart and anxiety not only affects our sleep, it damages our digestive tracks as well. Almost every day there's another study coming out proving how much our emotions affect our physical well-being.

Our inner energy is affected when we avoid our feelings too. I'm devoting all of Section 6 to this topic, so for now, I'll only say our aliveness, our life-force, is blocked when we avoid our feelings. We end up with low energy, perhaps even depressed.

---

[55] If you're not familiar with the scene, here it is: https://bit.ly/2F9EqoO

Finally, the lack of EQ is the root cause of almost all compulsive behaviors. Addictions to alcohol, love[56], shopping, porn and gambling, to name only a few, are ways we cope with deeply painful emotions that we're unwilling to face.

IT'S A HORRIBLE LIFE

Here's the bottom line: *If you want to feel good—if you want a wonderful life—then move towards your uncomfortable feelings, not away from them.* But if you want a horrible life, meaning, if you want relationship problems, if you want to be physically sick, if you want to feel energetically blocked, and if you want to be addicted, then move away from them.

Now, I'm pretty sure you want a wonderful life, so the first step towards that is to become aware of how you avoid your feelings. We all have our favorite avoidance strategy (or strategies). It's nothing to feel bad about. We all avoid our feelings in one way or another and to one degree or another, including me. But…

You can't learn how to be emotionally intelligent until you know how you're being emotionally UN-intelligent.

Here's an analogy. If you were to take a golf lesson, the first thing a good instructor would do is record your swing and show you what you're doing wrong. Once you see what not to do, you can then learn what you should do. It's the same way here. *Once you see what not to do with your feelings, then you can learn what you should do with them.* So, with the rest of this chapter, I'd like to describe 10 different ways we avoid our feelings— what not to do, in other words—and then in the final chapter of this section, I'll show you what you should do with your feelings.

---

[56] My first book, *A Drink with Legs*, is about love addiction.

10 WAYS WE AVOID FEELINGS

1. Distraction—The most common way we avoid our feelings is to distract ourselves from them. This is so habitual and ingrained, that half the time we don't even know we're doing it! When a feeling like loneliness or boredom comes up, we instinctively turn on the TV, or we grab our phones and scroll through Facebook, Instagram or Twitter. Some of us clean, engage in some hobby, surf the Internet or meditate (yes, even meditation can be a way to avoid our experience).

There are a million different ways we divert our attention away from an uncomfortable feeling. And some of them are very sneaky. On the surface, they look like perfectly innocent activities, even beneficial, (e.g., meditation), but underneath they can be done as a way to avoid a feeling. What's your favorite distraction activity? Mine is watching TV. I use it to distract myself from worry.

2. Medication—The second most common avoidance strategy is to medicate a feeling or numb it out. We do this with actual meds like pain killers, but we can do this with food (it's not called "comfort food" for nothing), exercise, marijuana, psychedelics, porn, romance novels, gambling, shopping, and of course, most people's favorite, alcohol. What's your favorite type of "Novocain"? Mine is *Grey Goose*. I often drink to numb my fear of failure.

3. Repression—While all 10 strategies are repression strategies, here I'm specifically referring to suppressive actions like withholding, denying, concealing, or saying "I'm fine." Also, whenever we're "being brave" or "keeping a stiff upper lip," or "hangin' in there," we are repressing a feeling. Even smiling, making jokes and praying can be ways we repress. How do you repress your feelings? One of my favorite ways is making jokes. I do it to repress sadness.

4. Venting—This one is a little tricky because on the surface it looks like we're releasing the feeling by venting to someone about it, but in reality, we're still not feeling our feelings directly. We're in our heads telling our story, whining and complaining about what someone did to us or about how life is unfair. That is not feeling an emotion, that is just "blowing off steam." It might temporarily relieve some internal pressure, but since the feeling isn't being contacted directly and allowed to tutor us toward some sort of life change, the feeling will just recycle and return, probably stronger than ever.

5. Blaming—Pointing the finger (usually the middle one) at someone and blaming them for our feelings is actually a sneaky way of avoiding them too. When we blame, our focus of attention is "out there" on whatever or whoever we believe has caused our feelings. This takes us away from our direct experience, puts us up in our heads and makes the feeling intensify, not dissolve. Blaming creates righteous indignation, not inner peace.

6. Analyzing—Trying to "figure it out" is a favorite strategy among personal development types. We love the "why" questions. But no amount of insight into the cause of a feeling has ever done anything to release it. For example, if your partner cheated on you, you know damn well why you feel sad and angry, don't you? They cheated on you! Does that knowledge do anything to release the feeling? Of course not.

And besides, accurately determining cause and effect is a very tricky endeavor, too. We've already talked about how warped and neurotic the Personal Mind is, so when you ask it for wisdom as to why you feel sad, angry or scared, you're asking for trouble. Whenever we experience uncomfortable feelings, we don't want to look up into our heads for answers, we want to look down into our bodies, feel the feeling, release it, and then learn from it. Analyzing is a waste of time and it won't make you feel better.

7. Explaining—A close cousin to analyzing is explaining. The former is a conversation you have with yourself, the latter is one you have with someone else. Neither is actually *feeling* the feeling, and both are a waste of time. However, I admit that talking about a feeling does seem to help and I'm not saying you should never do that. But I am saying that *before* you talk about your feelings, feel them.

And even then, if you listen closely to your words when you're telling your story, you'll hear that you're likely rationalizing, rehashing, excusing, defending, criticizing, justifying or judging—yourself or someone else. You won't feel better doing that.

"I've never seen anyone change their lives by talking about the past, and if you talk about it longer than ten minutes, you're wasting major time."
~ Dr. Gay Hendricks [57]

---

8. Apologizing—Many of us feel guilty, embarrassed or ashamed of our feelings. That probably comes from the way in which we were raised. And even if it does, it's time to stop apologizing for how we feel. Emotions aren't right or wrong, good or bad—even if someone tells us they are. They're our feelings, and there's nothing to apologize for. But when we choose to apologize for being upset, confused or frustrated, for example, we're

---

[57] *Conscious Living: Finding Joy in the Real World*, by Gay Hendricks. Note: He's a psychologist and said that!

rejecting ourselves and our current reality. And if we have people in our lives who insist that we apologize for how we feel, we need to get rid of them.[58]

9. Spiritualizing—This is maybe the trickiest one of all. Positive thinking, using affirmations, uttering spiritual platitudes or clichés, quoting scripture verses, etc.—as true as they may be in principle—are often sneaky ways we avoid our experience. Saying "God is in control" when someone you love dies, while true, is a way of avoiding the reality of your grief and anger. Remember, Jesus wept[59], and I'm pretty sure he knew God was in control. All that is to say, quit playing spiritual games and get real.

10. Acting Out—Whenever our core fears are triggered, the "fight or flight" dynamic sets in and we will act out compulsively and destructively. Listen to how Don Richard Riso and Rich Hudson describe it in their great book, *The Wisdom of the Enneagram*:

> "What is the difference between feeling an emotion and acting it out? If we feel angry, we can act it out by throwing a temper tantrum or we can resist the tendency and sit quietly with whatever we feel noting the sensations that anger causes in our bodies. When we do this, we have the opportunity to see on a deeper level what our feelings are about. This does not mean that we are suppressing our feelings. On the contrary, it means that we will actually feel them instead of letting them lead us into compulsive behavior."[60]

---

[58] I'm talking about feelings not behavior. If you *do* something harmful or hurtful *because* of the way you feel, you should definitely take responsibility for that and commit to a new way of behaving. But don't let anyone shame you for how you feel.

[59] John 11:35

[60] The Enneagram is THE best personal/spiritual growth tool I've ever come across and highly recommend that you study it and fall in love with it. Understanding your personality type is essential to all aspects of life, but it's especially helpful in intimate relationships. However, it's far too complex to discuss here, and frankly Riso and Hudson do a much better job of explaining it than I ever could. Therefore, I've referenced their book in Appendix I.

WORKOUT!

Those are the top 10 ways we avoid our feelings and here is a simple two-part "workout" to begin integrating this into your life:

1. Go through every one of the ten and identify how (not if) you do them in your life. Be very descriptive.
2. Before you turn the page and learn about how to feel your feelings, ask yourself this question (and "yes" or "no" are both perfectly acceptable):

Are you willing to stop avoiding your feelings in the ways you just identified?

(Note: I'm not asking you to be perfect. You will frequently fall back into avoiding your feelings. I know I do. I'm only asking if you are *willing* to commit to a new way of being with them, one that will create a wonderful life and not a horrible one.)

— 10 —

FEELINGS

&

What to Do When You're an Emotional Wreck

"Instead of resisting any emotion, the best way to dispel it is to enter it fully, embrace it and see through your resistance."

~ Deepak Chopra

All of what has been said up until now has been to prepare you for this moment. *What will you do when you're an emotional wreck?* Notice I didn't say *if* you're an emotional wreck, I said *when*. You're a human being so it's going to happen…All. The. Time. The question is, how are you going to respond? When you're hurt, lonely, sad, stressed or angry, for example, what will you do? This is where angels hold their breath.

By now, you are well aware that you only have two choices: You can either feel your feelings or you can avoid them—by using any one of the ten different avoidance strategies we discussed in the last chapter. And frankly, you will never choose to feel your feelings unless, and until, you are totally convinced that avoiding them not only doesn't work, but that it actually ruins your life.

But that is something you have to learn for yourself. Here's the truth: *I can tell you* that avoiding your feelings will ruin your chance at a truly authentic relationship. *I can tell you* that your body will get sick if you keep that energy trapped inside of you. *I can tell you* that avoiding your feelings is sucking the very life out of you. *I can tell you* that no matter what avoidance strategy you use, at best, it will only give you temporary relief. *I can tell you* that once you sober up (or finish the box of cookies, or put the phone down, or turn the TV off, etc., etc.) the feeling will return. *I can tell you* that feelings, when avoided, are like trick birthday candles that can't be blown out. The flame might disappear for a moment, but it will quickly reignite, requiring that you blow it out again and again and again—with your favorite avoidance strategy. *I can tell you* that this creates a vicious emotional loop, one that very often leads to addiction.

I can tell you all of that, but you have to see it for yourself. **In other words, you have to hit "rock bottom" and see from your own direct experience, that your way of being with your emotions isn't working.** That's the only way you'll be willing to try a different approach.

And if you are, what follows will truly change your life. But if you're not yet ready to commit to a new way of being with your emotions, that's OK. Read on anyway. At least you'll be familiar with how to feel a feeling if you do someday realize that avoiding them is ruining your life.

PATIENCE

Now, a couple of things to keep in mind as we proceed. First, because we've been using our favorite avoidance strategies for so long, they've become habits and those are hard to break. So be patient with yourself. This new path will not be easy.

Secondly, even when we are aware that we have a choice to feel or avoid our feelings, we may still choose to avoid them. Frankly, I do it all the time and I'm sure you will too. As strange as it sounds, you'll find that sometimes you actually want to stay stuck in a feeling or a mood rather than release it. It's bizarre, but it's true. And because it's true, the practice or technique I'm about to describe is best thought of as an *option*. It's available to us whenever we're willing to use it.

In other words, whenever we want to feel ecstatically alive, whole and connected to ourselves and everyone around us, we'll practice what's called, **"The 5 L's of EQ."** But when we'd rather stay stuck in some mood and mope around and feel upset, we can turn to our favorite avoidance strategy. *We get to choose our path, moment to moment.* And if you're like me, you'll yo-yo back and forth between the two. And that's OK. Again, be gentle with yourself and no matter what path you choose, do it with humor and self-acceptance.

Finally, learning "The 5 L's" is like learning to play the piano. It's a skill that requires practice. At first it will feel very awkward and you won't be very good at it, but if you keep "practicing your scales," one day you'll be able to play *Beethoven*. The same applies with your emotions. If you practice, one day you'll be very emotionally skilled; in fact, you'll be emotionally smarter than a 5th grader.[61]

THE 5 L's of EQ

Now that we've laid the groundwork, let's get back to our original question: *What do you do when you're an emotional wreck?* Well, first, determine if you're willing to feel that feeling and not avoid it. That's the key issue. And if you are, then find a quiet place, sit by yourself and *be with your experience,* for that's what it means to be emotionally intelligent.

Emotional Intelligence means to be with your experience, and The 5 L's are simply a structured, step-by-step way of doing that.[62]

---

[61] If you struggle with "The 5 L's" (or anything else in this book for that matter), reach out to me for individual coaching, or consider joining one of my *Online Relationship Bootcamps.* For information visit www.coachingwithroy.com or email me at coachingwithroy@gmail.com.

[62] At first it will have to be formal like this. Eventually, you'll be able to do this anywhere, even in the midst of a conversation, for you'll discover that when you develop this skill it only takes seconds to do.

The 5 L's don't need a lot of explanation because even a 5th grader can understand them, so I'll be brief. The only thing to keep in mind is that they must be done in order.

1. LABEL

The first step is simply to name the feeling you're experiencing and be sure to use the 5 primary emotions as labels (angry, sad, scared, joyful, sexual). Don't sugar-coat it by using some politically correct equivalent. Don't say, "I'm bummed out," say, "I feel sad." Don't say, "I'm ticked off," say, "I feel angry." Don't say, "I'm concerned," say, "I feel scared." Yes, there are degrees of sadness, anger and fear, but something magical happens when we refuse to image-manage, and instead, choose to speak the raw, real truth.[63]

2. LOCATE

Identify where the feeling is located in the body and describe what it's doing. For example, "I feel heaviness in my chest and it's hard to breathe," or "There's an aching, tight sensation in the back of my neck and across my shoulders," or "I feel a churning in my stomach." At the simplest level, this is what it means to *be with your experience.* Your attention is moving toward the feeling. You're not moving away from it by reaching for the wine bottle or checking Instagram.

These first two steps take a matter of seconds to do, and believe it or not, a shift can happen without doing steps 3-5. Sitting quietly and labeling and locating a feeling can have the same effect as picking up a crying baby. Both sometimes quiet down. However, if that doesn't happen, then move on to the third step.

---

[63] I am well aware that some spiritual teachers (e.g., Scott Kiloby) take exception to the naming of energies, believing that it's mind-made and unnecessary. And there's truth in that. However, since most people are so conditioned to avoid and suppress their feelings, labeling is a powerful and necessary step toward authenticity. Once you develop this skill, you will find step 1 unnecessary and even distracting.

3. LOVE

Loving a feeling is the true heart of this practice and it's the critical step to releasing most feelings. To love a feeling means to welcome it like you would your best friend showing up at your front door. *"Oh, I'm so glad to see you! Come in. Come in!"* It means to have a friendly, welcoming disposition toward your experience, no matter what it is. But unlike a friend that you might want to hang out with all day, with feelings, after you've experienced them fully, the idea is to open up the back door and let them go.

An emotionally intelligent person lives with their front AND back "doors" wide open. Feelings are welcomed in, they're experienced, and they are released.

If your "front door" is closed, you're avoiding your feelings. They aren't being allowed in and many of us live "closed" off to our experience. But if we do allow a feeling in (or if it breaks in—sometimes it feels like that, doesn't it?), many of us close the "back door." We won't let the feeling move all the way through us! We trap it inside and that's what causes all the harm we've been discussing. There's nothing wrong or dangerous about experiencing anger, sadness or fear. What's dangerous, what ruins us relationally, physically and energetically is not letting feelings go.

And letting feelings go (opening the back door, if you will) is done by *breathing, vocalizing and moving*. (Notice that *thinking* is not one of the steps. This not a head thing. It's all done in and from the body.)

> **3a. Breathing**—Most of us know we're supposed to breathe when we're upset, but here I'm talking about a more intentional kind of breathing, something called, *conscious breathing*. It's done by sending the breath, through imagination, to the exact location where the sensations are occurring in the body. For

example, if you feel angry and the back of your neck is tight (those are steps 1 & 2), sit quietly, and with every inhale, feel as though you're sending the breath directly to the back of your neck. In so doing, you're loving the feeling and giving it both permission to exist and the space to release.

3b. Vocalizing— Since emotion is merely energy trapped in the body, vocalizing a feeling often releases it. In other words, allow the energy to move out of the body—not with words!—but by making *sounds*. Ask yourself, "If this sensation/emotion could make a sound, what would it be?" Then let the feeling express itself through sound, only be sure that the sound matches the intensity of the emotion. In other words, if anger is present, make a big, loud, angry sound. *The expression must match the experience, or a release will not happen.* Jim Dethmer describes it this way:

> "We intuitively understand this because we see babies and animals do this all the time. Beings who aren't encumbered by the ability to think obsessively about feelings simply release them. Babies cry, dogs growl and cats hiss. They naturally match experience with expression and release emotion. Babies and animals don't hold on to feelings. They let them go."

3c. Moving—The final way energy is released from the body is through physical movement. Simply ask yourself, "If the sensation/emotion could move, how would it do that?" Then let the emotion take over your body and use it to express itself. But again, as with making sound, it's critical that the movement match the intensity of the feeling. So, if you're really angry, get a pillow and beat the crap out of it, while at the same time, making sound and breathing.

These three steps are what you do when you're an emotional wreck. This is how you "open the back door" and allow a feeling to move all the way through to completion. You Label, Locate and Love the feeling, and it takes less than 3 minutes to do. If you practice this regularly in your life, you will find it incredibly easy to shift out of emotional turmoil and return to a state of ease and flow.

But not always.

4. LOOK

Sometimes the "3 L's" don't work.

That's right, sometimes you can label a feeling and locate it in your body, then you can release that energy by breathing, vocalizing and moving, and still you might not experience a release. *When this happens, and it will, it means that the feeling was generated by a thought rather than an experience.* And as long as the thought is in place and believed to be true, "The 3 L's" won't help.

"Feelings are stories."
~ Jim Dethmer

For example, as I mentioned before, if you have the thought that you'll never meet someone special and that you're going to die alone, as long as you believe that to be true, you'll never stop feeling scared and sad. The feelings will morph into a ***mood***, a type of emotional straight-jacket from which you can't escape, even by using the first 3 "L's."

Therefore, a completely different approach is needed to release a thought-generated feeling. That brings us to the fourth "L," which is to **LOOK for the thought behind the feeling.** And the best technique I've ever come across to release thought-generated feelings is Byron Katie's, *The Work*. We've already talked about this amazing tool at the very end of Chapter 7, so I won't repeat myself here. I'll simply refer you to that section of the book. However, I will say that...

An emotionally intelligent person regularly practices *The Work* in their life.

In my experience, you have very little chance at real emotional freedom unless you use this tool in your life regularly. Every time you find yourself the least bit triggered or upset, stop and ask yourself what thought or belief is causing the upset and then do *The Work* on that thought. Ask yourself, *"Is that true? Can I absolutely know that it's true? and so on.*[64] *In* other words, if "the voice in the head" is going to talk to you all day, then at least make it talk about something that will make you feel better.

5. LEARN

The final step in feeling our feelings all the way through to completion is to learn from them. There is a wisdom in our feelings. They arise for a reason. Just as a fever indicates an infection, so an emotion often indicates that something is out of alignment in our lives and needs our attention.

But this step must always be done last. **You never want to seek the wisdom of an emotion when you're still in the grip of it.** When you're in a triggered and reactive state, you will almost always misinterpret what the feeling means and create more drama for yourself and everyone around you.

---

[64] There are 4 questions that comprise *The Work* and these are the first two. To learn more about this amazing tool, see: www.thework.com.

As an example, imagine that I spin you around until you're incredibly dizzy and then ask you to figure out 342 x 5 in your head. You couldn't do it, right? You'd say, "Give me a minute to get my bearings! I can't think straight right now, I'm too dizzy. Let me regain my balance and then I'll be able to think."

Well, that's what it's like when you're an emotional wreck. You're "dizzy" and unable to think straight. So, before you attempt to interpret the meaning of a feeling, and certainly before you take any sort of action, you must first release the emotion and regain your "balance." Otherwise, you're headed for trouble.

"Of all the advice in the world that you do not want to listen to, it is the advice of an emotionally disturbed mind."
~ Michael Singer

Once the inner turbulence has subsided and you're in a calm, centered state of consciousness, you can then learn from the feeling and seek its wisdom. And you will find that each of the five primary feelings has a particular message imbedded in them.[65]

- **ANGRY** means something wants to be stopped, changed or ended. When anger is governed and motivated by love and not ego, it's an energy that sets healthy boundaries, creates positive change and stands for a higher good.[66] In a sense, anger is like pruning a rose bush. In order for the bush to grow, the dead branches need to be cut away. Likewise, anger cuts

---

[65] An entire book could be written about each of the primary feelings and that's not my purpose here. I merely want to give you a basic understanding of what they mean, and if you have questions, I trust you'll reach out to me. Unlike many authors, I am available to my readers.
[66] Jesus is a great example of this. See, Matthew 21: 12-13

away anything that is inhibiting growth in our lives or in the lives of those we care about. So, when anger comes up in you, once you've released it by using "The 3 L's," or by doing *The Work* on the thought that created it, ask yourself, "What needs to be stopped, changed or ended?"

- **SAD** means something wants to be let go of, mourned or said goodbye to. It's an energy of loss. So, when you feel sad, ask yourself, "What am I holding on to that I need to let go of?" Now, when sadness is experience-generated (e.g., the loss of a relationship, someone dies, you lose a job, etc.), the feeling may come in waves, and if we use "The 3 L's" for each wave, those feelings will move through us very quickly.[67] But if the sadness stays around for weeks, months or even years, it's being generated by a thought, perhaps something like, "He should not have left me," or "I should be married by now," or "She should not have died." Those thoughts are not true (he did leave you, you're not married, and she did die), but as long as you believe those thoughts are true, as long as you're arguing with *"what is,"* your sadness will become a dark, sticky mood and you're headed for depression. For those kinds of feelings, the quickest way out is doing *The Work*.

- **SCARED** means something wants to be known or requires your full attention. Think of a deer in the woods that hears a sound. It comes to absolute presence with its eyes wide open. Fear says, "Wake up! Get here right now and pay attention." The odd thing about fear is that you can be scared about something real or something imagined. For example, if you're about to cross a busy street, there's a real fear of getting hit by a car. In that case, your fear says, "Pay attention!" That's an experienced-

---

[67] Sadness seems to be the only feeling that comes in waves. Initially the waves come close together, and over time, the space out until they're gone.

generated fear and you better listen to it. But many of our fears are thought-generated stories about the future. It's the Personal Mind running wild, imagining worst case scenarios and telling stories of doom. It's not about something real, something that's here and now. It's about "what if's." *What if I never meet someone? or What if my company down-sizes and I lose my job? or What if I get sick and there's no one to take care of my kids?* Those are thoughts, and they shouldn't be listened to. Instead, you should do *The Work* on them.

• **JOYFUL** means something wants to be celebrated. At first glance, you might think we do this one fairly well. But I'm not so sure. Yes, if our team wins or if our kids get straight "A's," we celebrate. But how often do we truly appreciate the people around us, both for what they do and who they are? Seems to me that we spend a lot more time criticizing and judging than we do celebrating and appreciating. Don't you spend more time condemning yourself than you do congratulating yourself? Joy means something wants to be celebrated. What is that? Who is that?

• **SEXUAL** feelings mean something wants to be created, birthed or brought into existence. It's the energy of procreation, obviously, but it's so much more than that. It's the life-force, the very energy behind the impulse to create anything.

Many people reading this book don't have a partner in their life, yet they still have a lot of sexual energy running in their bodies. It's a pressure that seems to have no outlet and it can be quite frustrating. But the emotionally intelligent single person doesn't necessarily relieve or discharge that pressure through masturbation or meaningless sexual activity. Nor do they trap and suppress it in their bodies. They, instead, use that energy to fuel their entire lives, channeling it into their priorities and passions. They choose to have sex with life, in a sense, directing their sexual energy into the way they workout, play with their kids, make sales calls or write a book.

I'm not saying there is anything morally wrong with masturbating or casual sex. I've done a lot of one and a little of the other. What you do with your body is your business. But have you noticed that after an orgasm, you don't have a lot of energy to workout, take your kid to the park or sit with a person in need? Don't drain yourself of sexual energy nonchalantly. It's the life-force and the source of your creativity. Expend it intelligently.

WORKOUT!

What do you do when you're an emotional wreck? You Label, Locate, Love, Look and Learn from your feelings. That's EQ. And the "workout" is simple. *Just do it.*

To close out this section of the book, here's a poem by *Rumi*, a 13th century mystic. It beautifully captures the essence of what it means to be emotionally intelligent.

GUEST HOUSE
This being human is a guest house
Every morning a new arrival.
A joy, a depression, a meanness,
some momentary awareness comes
as an unexpected visitor.
Welcome and entertain them all!
Even if they are a crowd of sorrows,
who violently sweep your house
empty of its furniture,
still treat each guest honorably.
He may be clearing you out for some new delight.
The dark thought, the shame, the malice,
meet them at the door laughing,
and invite them in.

Be grateful for whoever comes,
Because each has been sent
as a guide from beyond.

WORKOUT #4

STRENGTHENING YOUR RELATIONSHIP TO THE PAST

HOLD ON or LET GO

"Remember this: 100% of spiritual growth, development and unfoldment is about letting go of something; it's not about getting or acquiring something. It's about releasing something."
~ Michael Bernard Beckwith

156

— 11 —

THE PAST

&

The Importance of a Clean Emotional Slate

"As I walked out the door toward my freedom, I knew that if I did not leave all the anger, hatred and bitterness behind that I would still be in prison."
~ Nelson Mandela [68]

I've had two great passions in my life: personal growth and competitive golf. In fact, they've been so important to me that for more than 30 years, they've been professions of mine. Since the early 1980's, I've been supporting people's growth in some capacity and I've also been a professional golfer since then, too.[69] I have literally spent almost my entire adult life attempting to understand the keys to success in those two areas. And if there's one thing I've learned over the years it's that *success in either is largely determined by how you deal with the past.*

For instance, in golf, everyone hits bad shots no matter how good they are. And if you don't let go of those bad shots, if you hold on to your anger or upset and don't approach the next shot with *a clean emotional slate*, that next shot is likely to be just as bad or even worse than the previous one.

---

[68] Nelson Mandela was imprisoned for 27 years (1962-1989) in a South African prison for his leadership of the anti-apartheid movement.
[69] In terms of personal development, I've been a pastor, speaker, teacher, author and coach, and in golf, I've played in 76 PGA Tour events, including 7 major championships, and I've won more than 80 tournaments over the life of my career (though none on the PGA Tour).

So, if you want to play your best golf, you have to let go of the *recent* past (the previous shot) but you also have to let go of the *distant* past, too. As strange as this may sound, it's not uncommon for a golfer to be *traumatized* by something that happened years or even decades ago. If you hit a terrible shot or miss an important putt, even if it happened a long time ago, it can leave a mark on your soul. You can feel permanently damaged in some way, like it alters your very identity and you end up thinking of yourself as "the golfer that choked under pressure."[70] If this happens, it's sure to sabotage your future performance.

To be successful in golf, then, you must let go of the past, whether it's three minutes ago or three decades ago. *You must learn from your bad shots, release any emotional residue they have left behind, and move on, putting all your attention on the present.* But if you hang on to any negativity from the recent or distant past, you're ruining not only your next shot (and perhaps the whole round), but maybe even your entire career.

The same is true in relationships.

It's quite possible that you've been hurt recently. Perhaps you were betrayed, deceived, played, ghosted or dumped. No matter what it was, if you don't approach the next relationship with *a clean emotional slate*, you will either build a wall around your heart, one that will keep you safe (and single), or you will poison a new relationship with your baggage and prevent it from becoming the beautiful intimacy it could be. Hanging on to anger, hatred and bitterness only sabotages your ability to create a healthy relationship in the future. So, you have to let go of the *recent* past. But like golf, you also have to let go of the *distant* past.

It's not uncommon for a person to be *traumatized* by something that happened years or even decades ago. If a person was abused or abandoned,

---

[70] In 1989, Scott Hoch missed a two-foot putt to win the *Masters*. Although he played some good tournaments after that, he never really recovered. Here's the video of that putt: https://bit.ly/2CIHFRh

or if they grew up around addiction, that can leave a mark on the soul, especially if it happened in their childhood. They can feel permanently damaged, like it altered their very identity and now they think of themselves as "the one who's unworthy or unlovable."

Success in relationships, therefore, is largely about letting go of the past, whether it was three minutes or three decades ago. *It's about learning from your past experiences, releasing any emotional residue they've left in their wake and moving on with an open, available heart.* But hanging on to negativity ruins not only your next relationship, but perhaps even all of your future relationships.

HOLD ON or LET GO?

In this section of the book, we are going to focus on strengthening your relationship to the past, and the choice that we're going to explore is whether we will *hold on* to the past or *let go* of it. And I fear that there's going to be a strong temptation to skip this "workout" because the past feels either too painful to face or utterly impossible to release (or both). If you feel that way, I completely understand. But letting go does NOT mean rehashing and reliving your past pain, nor does it mean forgetting what happened, because that is impossible.

Letting go is an on-going process (not a one-time event) that includes: (1) learning from the past, (2) releasing any emotional residue it created, and (3) opening our hearts to the present moment.

SNEAK PREVIEW

To do that, we have to engage in some "hard-core training," which means talking about those three very uncomfortable subjects, all of which will be covered in this section. First, in order to learn from the past, we have to talk about *responsibility and blame*. Second, in order to release the emotional residue created by our past experiences, we have to talk about *regret and forgiveness*. And third, if we are to open (or re-open) our hearts, if we are to pursue intimacy with a clean emotional slate, we have to talk about *triggers and trust*.

This is the most challenging part of the entire book, and because of that, we need to be totally convinced that these three "workouts" are absolutely necessary, otherwise we won't be willing to do them. Therefore, here is a brief discussion of five very dangerous results of holding on to the past.

FIVE DANGERS OF HOLDING ON

1. Projection

Imagine that you're wearing a pair of stylish sunglasses that are tinted a pale shade of yellow. Everything will look a little yellow, right? But that's not a problem because you know the sunglasses are distorting reality. So, if you were to meet someone while wearing your sunglasses, they would look a little yellow to you, but you wouldn't actually think they were suffering from jaundice, you'd know it's just the sunglasses that make them look that way. And because you know that, you're free to get to know them for who they are and not who they appear to be.

But when you hold on to the past, it's like you're wearing sunglasses—*tinted in the shade of your pain*—but you don't know you're wearing them! Therefore, you are ***not*** free to see someone for who they truly are, you're seeing them through the lens of your past and projecting that on to them. In other words, any potential partner looks a little "yellow" to you, meaning, **they look like another person who will hurt you in the same way others have.**

Here's the problem this creates: Any person worth their salt is going to pick up on your projection and resent that they are being judged by someone else's behavior. In the end, seeing potential partners through the lens of your past is a sure way to keep yourself single.

2. Protection

In order to experience a deeply connected intimate relationship, your heart has to be open and accessible. Metaphorically speaking, we can't be protecting our hearts with arms crossed, they have to be wide open to life and love. But when the pain is still alive in us, we not only close our hearts, we also become unnecessarily skeptical and suspicious, too scared to let a relationship progress at a natural pace. In other words, we might go too slow (if we allow a relationship to happen at all!), or perhaps even question a person's motives if they seem too eager to connect with us. All of this is a huge turn off! As I said earlier, walls keep you safe, but they keep you single.

3. Presentation

You've probably heard the saying, "you can run, but you can't hide." That's true in this discussion. We can run from the past, but we can't hide it. The longer you hold on to something, the more it shows up in your physical presentation. *In other words, we become what we hold on to.* If we hold on to anger, hatred and bitterness, we will become angry, hateful, bitter people—and others will see and feel it.

Our physical bodies reveal our inner realities. This is the reason why a Polygraph test works and it's also why good poker players can pick up on their opponents "tells." **If we're holding on to the past, there's no way to hide that from others.** It will show up in our affects, attitudes, actions and of course, our words. And need I say, no one is attracted to "Suspicious Suzy" or "Angry Andy."

4. Patterns

In the movie, *Groundhog Day*, Bill Murray plays a character who is stuck living the same day over and over again until he makes peace with it.[71] The movie beautifully illustrates a profound truth. We will experience the same partners, patterns, problems and pain—over and over again—until we make peace with the past. As Winston Churchill famously said, "Those who do not learn from history are doomed to repeat it."[72] How true that is in our love lives! The past is magnetic, so unless you want to end up in "Relationship Groundhog Day," you better do the "hard-core training" it takes to let go of the past.

5. Power

The final result of holding on to the past is that it reduces our attraction power.[73] What makes a masculine person truly attractive is when they are *present*, meaning they're living a life of clarity, responsiveness and openness. But when a masculine person is living in the past, their presence-power is *weakened* and they are experienced as being confused, distracted and closed—all of which are total turn-offs to feminine people.

Likewise, what makes a feminine person attractive is when they are *radiant*, meaning they are living a life of sensuality, vulnerability and playfulness. But when a feminine person can't let go of the past, their radiance-power is *darkened*, and they are experienced as being stiff, guarded and serious—all of which are total turn-offs to masculine people.[74]

---

[71] If you aren't familiar, enjoy: http://bit.ly/1lZC4Ll
[72] While Churchill made the statement famous in 1948, it was first said by George Santayana in 1905.
[73] This subject is fully explored in *Section 6: Strengthening Your Relationship to Your Inner Energy*
[74] Notice I'm not talking about genders, but energies. More about this in Section 6 of this book but you can also learn more about this topic in Section 6 of *Attracting Lasting Love*, my previous book.

WORKOUT!

After reading about those five dangers, I hope you are sufficiently convinced to do whatever it takes to let go of the recent or distant past. **Just as a hot-air balloon cannot fly as long as it's tethered to the ground, so your love life cannot soar as long as you're tethered to the past.** You must cut the cords to the past, and the remaining chapters in this section of the book will show you how to do that.

But before you turn the page, do the following short "workout." Look at the dangers discussed in this chapter and pick the one(s) that you feel most hinders your love life and answer its question.

1. **Projection**: Who have you projected your past on to and what effect did (does) it have on the relationship?

2. **Protection**: If there's a wall around your heart, how would a potential partner experience that? In other words, what does your wall feel like to others?

3. **Presentation**: What specific ways (attitude, action, affect, words) do you reveal that you've not let go of your past pain?

4. **Pattern**: What pattern continues to repeat in your life and how does that remind you of the past?

5. **Power**: Describe the specific ways your presence or radiance is diminished because you're holding on to the past.

— 12 —

THE PAST

&

The Payoffs of Not Letting Go

"I have little use for the past and rarely think about it."
~ Eckhart Tolle

Many smokers find it very difficult to quit. I know that was true of my parents. They were both life-long smokers and they tried to quit many times, but never did. It wasn't that they didn't know *how* to quit—all you do is stop putting cigarettes in your mouth—it was that they were *unwilling* to quit. Even after heart attacks and by-pass surgeries, neither one of them stopped smoking. They just didn't want to quit.

The same is true when it comes to letting go of the past. While the "how" part of letting go is a bit more complicated than just not putting cigarettes in your mouth, when it comes right down to it, if we have trouble letting go of the past, it's not so much because we don't know *how* to let go, it's because we're *unwilling* to let go.

That's why I spent the entire last chapter focusing on the importance of letting go. I showed that holding on to the past damages us relationally but I didn't even mention the toll it takes on us physically and emotionally. Every day there seems to be another study showing how the body is damaged when we hold on to anger and bitterness. And the very existence of pharmaceutical companies is largely the result of our collective commitment to not letting go of the past.

Yet even though we know that keeping the past alive is slowly killing us, much like smoking does, why are we frequently unwilling to let go? This is THE question. If we don't fully face *the willingness issue*, any discussion of *how* to let go will be a waste of time. So, here are three reasons why we are often unwilling to let go of the past.

THREE PAYOFFS OF NOT LETTING GO

1. The Past is Our "Brand"

Every business, from large corporations to individual entrepreneurs, seek to establish a unique, recognizable brand. *A brand is something you're known for.* It's a defining characteristic, something that sets you apart and makes you special. Without a brand or an identity, a company is basically invisible. Therefore, businesses of any size are incredibly invested in creating and promoting their brand. Their very existence depends on it.

The same is true of us. We, too, want to be known for something. We want a "personal brand" you could say, a defining characteristic, something that sets us apart and makes us special. That can be an accomplishment, a profession or even a possession. *But for many, our brand, what makes us special, is what's happened to us in the past.*

The truth is, we build an entire identity out of the past. It defines who we are, and it becomes what we're known for. And on top of that, whether we've experienced abuse, infidelity, deception, or any painful thing like that, we get an incredible amount of attention and sympathy because of it.

Therefore, we have a huge stake in keeping the past alive, for who would we be without our story? Would we matter? Would anyone care about us? Would anyone find us interesting? Would we become invisible? The answers to those questions are too terrifying to consider, so we won't allow ourselves to let go of the past. This is, perhaps, the most powerful payoff for holding on. It's just too risky to let go (this is where Byron Katie's, *The Work*, will come in handy. I've referenced this amazing tool a few times already in this book, and I'm wondering…are you using it?[75]).

2. We Are Addicted to Drama

Have you watched shows like *The Bachelor, Keeping Up with the Kardashians* or *Big Brother?* The people on those shows love drama, and frankly, so do those who watch it. There's a palpable adrenaline rush that comes from drama (blame, conflict, wanting to be right, etc.) and the truth is, it's addicting. We just love it, and letting go of the past means letting go of drama.

We love reliving the past, telling our story and blaming the bastard or bitch that is responsible for our pain. It's a reliable way to (temporarily) feel a surge of intoxicating energy in our bodies. In other words, drama feels good. It's not unlike what a drug addict experiences when they shoot up. *Can you believe what they did to me? They are such an asshole! I would never do something like that. What an f-ing liar they are!* Oh, God, it feels good to rant about the past.

But letting go is no fun because it puts an end to all that. There's no adrenaline rush in letting go. Therefore, we don't want to let go of the past no matter how much it damages us relationally, physically or emotionally. The truth is, we get far too much juice from it.

3. Misery Loves Company

It's quite common to connect with people, and perhaps even build an entire social circle with those who can relate to our pain (e.g., a divorce recovery group). It's very true that "misery loves company," and at least

---

[75] As you will hear throughout this book, if you need support in using this tool, or with anything else in this book, join one of my *Online Relationship Bootcamps* or work directly with me. For info visit, www.coachingwithroy.com or email me at: coachingwithroy@gmail.com

initially, that's not necessarily a bad thing. When we are first coming to grips with a painful past, whether it was abuse, infidelity, a break-up or some other kind of painful situation, it is extremely important to be supported by others who understand and share our pain. *But often, that pain becomes the basis of the friendship and the past is pretty much all you ever talk about.*

Therefore, letting go of the past—which means, at a minimum, to stop talking about it all the time—jeopardizes our social circles. If we let go of the past, we might not have anything else in common with our friends, and that can be enough to keep us from letting go.

WORKOUT!

I have now spent two entire chapters devoted to explaining how important it is to let go of the past and why we often don't. And frankly, there is nothing more I can do. Either you're willing to let go or you're not. If you are, the next couple of chapters will be life-changing for you. If you're not, they will be meaningless. So, it's your choice: *Hold On,* or *Let Go.*

But because I'm an optimist, I'm choosing to believe you're ready to let go. So, before I show you how to do that, do the following "workout." In your journal, answer the following three questions:

1. What are you known for? In other words, what is your "brand"? Describe it this way: "I am the one who _____ (fill in the blank). For example, *"I am the one who always gets ghosted, or I am the one who attracts unavailable men, or I am the one who gets cheated on, or I am the one who no one finds attractive."* In other words, what story of the past do you find yourself repeatedly telling anyone who will listen?

2. Who is mostly to blame for your pain, and what are you "right" about concerning that situation? For example, in my case, it was,

"My ex-wife is to blame, and I'm right that our sex life was her fault."

3. What connections would you lose (or fear you'd lose) if you refused to talk about your (or their!) past anymore? Are you willing to discuss this with them and see if your relationship can be reorganized around a healthier purpose or if it should be dissolved?

— 13 —

THE PAST

&

The Untethered Soul

"The national pastime, most people's favorite hobby, is collecting bad experiences. You are literally full of shit."

~ Michael Singer

The Untethered Soul is both the title of my favorite book and the ultimate goal of a conscious person's life. When it's all said and done, if our spirituality has any value at all, it must show us how to be liberated from the past and all the patterns, projections, personas and pain it creates, freeing us to respond to the present moment with an open and available heart. In other words, it must show us how to have an untethered soul.

Now that we've established how important it is to have a clean emotional slate and discussed a few powerful reasons why we're often unwilling to let go, we can now answer the "how" question. How can we let go of the past and quit carrying around all that painful baggage?

Well, as I've alluded to, the first step is learning from the past. Einstein reportedly said, *"Insanity is doing the same thing over and over again and expecting different results."* So, unless we're insane and want to live in our own versions of "Relationship Groundhog Day," experiencing the same patterns and pain over and over again, we need to learn from the past so that we aren't doomed to repeat it.

CONVICTION & CURIOSITY

But let's admit something right up front. Many of us don't think there's anything to learn from the past. We know what happened. We know who did what, we know the pain that was caused and the damage that was done, and we most certainly know whose fault it was. So, what's to learn? In our minds, it's cut and dry. *"I'm right and they're wrong. I'm the victim and they are the villain. They abandoned me. They hurt me. They cheated on me. They lied to me. They did this or that "to me."* So, when we have it all figured out like that, when we have that kind of conviction about what happened, what's to learn?

If the first step in letting go is learning from the past, we have to deal with how "right" we feel about what happened. In other words, as long as we're still blaming someone for what happened, we'll never be able to let go.

Blame is *THE* cord that keeps us tethered to the past. As long as we maintain the conviction that we are right and they are wrong, as long as we point the finger of blame and say, "This is your fault! You did this to me," we will never be free of the past.

Blame keeps the past alive.

It's said that "time heals all wounds." That is fundamentally not true. Time has no effect on blame. For example, if I blame my first wife for our failed marriage because she didn't want to have sex, how does time heal that? As long as I hold that conviction, the past stays alive in me. In other words, if it *was* her fault, it will *always* be her fault.

So, if we're going to let go of the past, we have to stop blaming and being right, and instead choose to be genuinely curious about how we were responsible for what happened in the past.

Taking radical responsibility is the only path to an untethered soul.

IT'S YOUR MOVIE

You'll recall that back in Chapter 3, we said that there are two basics ways to view life. You can either see yourself as a victim and believe things happen "to me," or you can see yourself as a creator and believe things happen "by me." We said that life is like a movie. You're either in someone else's movie, where you don't have any say in what happens, or it's your movie—you are the director, script writer and casting agent—and therefore, you have total control over everything that happens.

So, how do you view your life? Are you in someone else's movie, or are you responsible for everything that has happened in your life? In other words, did the past happen "to me" or "by me"? **How you answer that question determines whether you will be able to let go of the past and live with an open, available heart, or whether you will remain tethered to the past and probably recreate the same relationship dynamics over and over again.**

I'm guessing something in you bristles at what I'm suggesting. We love to blame. We love to point the finger at everyone but ourselves. Our egos refuse to entertain the possibility that we played a part in what happened, and that without that part, things could never have turned out as they did. In fact, you might be saying, *"How dare you suggest that what happened was my fault!"*

Well, I'm actually not suggesting it was your fault, nor am I saying it was their fault either, whoever "they" are. What I am saying—and we'll explore this more deeply in the next chapter—is that no one is at fault. *Everyone involved was unconsciously caught in the trance of their past conditioning, and together, the entire experience was co-created.*

MAKING STEW

In that sense, the past and whatever happened, is like a really nasty tasting stew. Everyone's psychological junk gets mixed together—the childhood patterns, the personality's blind spots, the fear-driven personas—all those "ingredients" create a nasty "stew" called the past.

The key to letting go, then, is learning what "ingredients" you put in the "stew," and realizing that without what you put in, the "stew" could never have tasted like it did. In other words, without your part, the relationship would never have gone as it did.

Here's an example from my life.

If you've read any of my previous books, you know I had a pattern of attracting women that were damsels in distress—women who felt completely overwhelmed by their lifestyles. They had very busy and successful careers, usually working 60-80 hours a week, and they were also single moms trying to care for their kids and manage their households.

The best example of this was my ex-fiancée, Julie.[76]

I enjoyed taking care of Julie and her life situation for a while, but eventually the relationship fell apart and I blamed her for it. There was no time for us, and I resented being forced into a "Mr. Mom" role because she chose to be a workaholic. Even years after that relationship ended, I still couldn't let go of my anger and resentment. I felt incredibly "right" about it being her fault.

The breakthrough came when I chose to be curious about how I was responsible for creating the rescuer/damsel dynamic. I saw that it was all about my relationship with my mother. The only time I received attention and affection from her was when I was being a good boy, meaning, when I was taking care of her and doing whatever it took to make her happy.

---

[76] I go into great detail about this relationship in my first book, *A Drink with Legs.*

No wonder I was attracted to damsels in distress! I was playing out my childhood pattern!

Once I saw this, how could I blame Julie (or any damsel) anymore? The script in my movie called for women to play the role of "Debbie the Damsel" so that I could play my role as "Roy the Rescuer." So, none of it was the women's fault. But it wasn't my fault either, for at the time, I was completely unaware of the pattern that was running my life.

The point is, none of it could have happened without my unconscious need to rescue women as a means of getting their attention and affection. And the same type of thing is responsible for your past and all the pain you've experienced. I don't care if you've been through infidelity, deception or some other type of betrayal. I don't care if your blame is directed towards a former lover, friend, coworker or family member. If you're willing to become curious about your childhood patterns, your personality's blind spots and your fear-driven personas, then you, too, will discover exactly what I did—that without your "ingredients," the relationship could never have gone as it did.

That doesn't mean people haven't done shitty things. Of course they have. Remember, relationship drama is always co-created. Everyone involved is equally responsible for what's happened. *But when you are willing to take radical responsibility, you recognize that without your part, without the "ingredients" you put in the "stew," it could never have turned out as it did.*

CHILDHOOD ABUSE

Whenever there's a discussion about responsibility and the "to me" vs. "by me" mindsets, the issue of childhood abuse (or any sort of childhood trauma) always comes up. Is a child responsible for being abused? Did they choose their alcoholic or drug-addicted parents? Did they choose to be abandoned and neglected? Of course not. No child is responsible for any of that. They truly are victims.

However, the adult who suffered that kind of trauma as a child is responsible for how they handle it now. Millions of people were (and are) dealt a horrible set of cards, and they deserve an incredible amount of understanding and compassion as a result. To personally experience abuse, abandonment or addiction at an early age can and does leave a mark on the soul. No one disputes that. But in the end, as challenging as it is, no matter what's happened in the past, we are responsible for how much we allow it to impact our lives now.

"Nothing ever happened in the past that can prevent you from being present now; and if the past cannot prevent you from being present now, what power does it have?"
~ Eckhart Tolle

HOW TO LET GO

Ok, let's get to it. If you are willing to shift out of blame and choose instead to be curious about how you are responsible for what's occurred, then you need to face three things concerning the past: (1) The Part You Played, (2) The Persona You Animated, and (3) The Payoff You Receive.

Each one, you'll notice, comes with a powerful question to help you let go. Wonder about each question for as long as it takes, which might be days or even weeks.

1. THE PART YOU PLAYED — *How was I responsible for what happened?*

This is the most fundamental question a "by me" person asks: "How did I create my experience?" To answer that question, I recommend a very playful yet powerful exercise called, *"Teaching Your Drama Class."*[77] If you are willing to take radical responsibility, it's an extremely effective tool. (If you're not, it won't make any sense to you and it may even piss you off.) Here's how it works:

a. First, name the issue from the past that you haven't been able to let go of. In other words, who are you blaming and for what? (For the sake of discussion, let's say you blame your ex for cheating on you.)

b. Second, imagine that you have been hired by a university to teach a class of students how to have the EXACT same experience you've had. (After all, you're the expert. It's already happened in your life, so it should be easy for you to teach others how to have it happen in theirs.)

c. Third, give your class a title. In our example it would be, "How to Get Cheated On."

d. Fourth, using the questions below as prompts, teach your students how to get cheated on by telling them the things you did to get cheated on:

    • What actions did you take (or not take), or what did you do (or not do) that led to what happened in the past?

    • What did you believe about yourself, others, relationships or the world that led to your experience?

    • What feelings did you repress, conceal or ignore?

---

[77] This exercise was developed by Jim Dethmer and Diana Chapman, of *The Conscious Leadership Group*. You can learn about them and their brilliant work at www.conscious.is

- What did you not say or speak up about that directly led to the past occurring as it did?

- What did you try to control that was not yours to control?

- What were you wanting to be right about?

- What "shoulds" did you have to believe?

- What story or belief did you hold about the issue?

- How did you try to fix the issue, but only in a temporary way?

- What did you have to be afraid of or choose not to face?

- What agreements did you make (or break) with yourself or others?

2. THE PERSONA YOU ANIMATED — *Who did I have to be in order for the past to occur?*

The second thing you need to face in order to let go of the past is something called your *relationship persona*.[78] A persona is not the real you, but the "person" you become, or a role you play, in order to get the love and attention you desire.

My relationship persona was "Roy the Rescuer."[79] Once I saw that he required women to be "damsels in distress" so that he could rescue them, I could no longer blame the "damsels" for being exactly what I needed—women who needed rescuing! I was responsible for the whole dynamic. This recognition cuts the cord of blame, and without blame, letting go happens effortlessly.

Now it's your turn. What persona were you animating that required your partners to be exactly as they were? Remember, personas are always

---

[78] For a complete and thorough discussion of relationship personas, see chapters 15-18 in my second book, *Attracting Lasting Love.*
[79] I call him "Casanova" in my other books. Both names refer to the same dynamic, it's just that "Roy the Rescuer" requires less explanation.

attracted to their reciprocal, matching opposites. There's a "cookies and milk" dynamic involved. So, for example, we've already seen that rescuers require damsels, and vice versa. They go together. Here are some other examples. Perhaps one will resonate with you and help you see how you were responsible for what happened in the past.

- "Charlie the Control Freak" requires "Donna the Doormat," and vice versa.
- "Paul the Player" requires "Grace the Gullible," and vice versa.
- "Annie the Addict" requires "Eddie the Enabler," and vice versa.
- "Nancy the Nurse" requires "Wally the Wounded," and vice versa.
- "Fred the Firefighter" requires "Doris the Drama Queen," and vice versa.
- "Ned the Narcissist" requires "Suzy the Self-Forgetter," and vice versa.

Notice how they are all perfect matches for each other. *They require each other.* But notice, too, that if you weren't caught in your persona, the whole dynamic would fall apart. In other words, if you weren't "Donna the Doormat," "Charlie" couldn't control you. Knowing that, how can you blame "Charlie?" And how could you blame yourself? You didn't know you were being "Donna." You were unconsciously caught in a childhood pattern, as I was, being the "person" and playing the role you thought you needed to play in order to make a relationship work. When you see this, letting go of the past happens effortlessly.

3. THE PAYOFF YOU RECEIVE — *What I get by continuing to hold on is...?*

The third thing we need to face is the hidden benefit or payoff we get for holding on to the past and keeping it alive. In other words, there's a reason we don't let go of the past. There's a payoff. What is it? Do you get a sense of identity from the past, as we talked about in the last chapter? Do you get a ton of attention and sympathy because of what happened? Does blaming them allow you to feel superior and "better than" they are?

Here's something very few people consider: Does not letting go keep you from having to take responsibility for your life now? In other words, do you use the past as an excuse or to justify your current life situation?

- "Given what I've been through, I can't help but have trust issues."
- "With my past, I can't help but be afraid of intimacy."
- "Knowing how I've been treated, I can't help but be suspicious and jaded."
- "With what happened to me, I can't help but be depressed."
- "Because of my past, I can't help but be an alcoholic."

What's your payoff for holding on?

BE BRAVE

It takes a truly brave soul to choose curiosity and learning over conviction and being right. It takes an even braver soul to put an end to blame and take radical responsibility for their past. To do so feels like you're losing yourself and letting the other win. And, to the ego, that's true. But do you want to be "right," or do you want to be free? Do you want to blame, or do you want an untethered soul?

I close this very challenging chapter with an amazing poem written by the 14th century mystic poet, *Hafiz*:

LOSING YOURSELF

To really lose yourself is like holding a gun to your head
And pulling the trigger—it takes courage.
Facing the truth means tying a bag over your head
Until you suffocate—it takes faith.
You have to be brave to follow God's tracks into the unknown
Where so many new things overwhelm and panic you.
But trust me and plunge the jeweled dagger into your heart.
This is what it takes to lose yourself.
There is no other path to God.

WORKOUT!

If you've answered the three questions above, I think you've done enough for one day, don't you?

— 14 —

THE PAST

&

How to Experience Forgiveness

"Father, forgive them; for they do not know what they are doing."
~ Jesus of Nazareth

Taking radical responsibility turns the whole idea of forgiveness on its ear.

Who is there to forgive if I'm responsible for the "stew"? Or to use our other metaphor, if life is my movie, if things don't happen "to me" but "by me," how could it be their fault and how could they need to be forgiven? The only person that could possibly need to be forgiven is me for writing the movie as I did.

The fact is, when we begin to look closely at our past, the whole thing begins to feel like a huge, emotional mess. Seeing our part in how our relationships went often creates an overwhelming amount of self-blame and regret, and if we're honest, we still feel a lot of anger and resentment about their part, too.

That was certainly true in my case. After seeing that "Roy the Rescuer" required me to attract "Debbie the Damsel" and that none of it could have happened without me being caught in my past conditioning, I felt a lot of self-blame and regret. Yet I still resented Julie for being a workaholic and taking advantage of me. My thinking was, *"Yes, I know what I did, but that's still no excuse for what she did!"*

In other words, having an *intellectual* understanding of how the past was co-created often doesn't release the *emotional* part. There is still a lot of emotional residue that seems stuck and Velcro-ed to our souls. Therefore...

To have a clean emotional slate means not only letting go *intellectually*, by understanding our part, it also means to let go *emotionally* by releasing any emotional charge that remains.

This is especially true in the case of childhood trauma. While there is no *intellectual* piece to understand—the child played no part in what happened—there sure is an *emotional* piece to release. When children experience (or witness) abuse, abandonment or addiction in their early years, there is often a tremendous amount of emotional residue left over from that.

For all these reasons, we need to have a serious conversation about the emotional residue the past often leaves behind, for we will never experience the joy of an untethered soul as long as it remains.

FORGIVENESS FALACIES

In my opinion, no spiritual topic is more misunderstood than is the topic of forgiveness. First of all, as was mentioned above, if you feel the need to forgive someone in the first place, that means you're still blaming them for what happened and you're not taking responsibility. From that perspective, you'll never let go of the past and you'll remain bitter, angry and hateful forever (nor will you learn anything).

Another fallacy about forgiveness is that it means you're supposed to forget what happened. But that's crazy. Forgiveness doesn't require some sort of spiritual lobotomy where your memory is removed. Nor does it mean putting your head in the sand, singing kumbaya, and denying what happened. People do shitty things and we do shitty things. There's no forgetting this or denying it. If someone cheated, they cheated. If someone lied, they lied. If someone abused, they abused. And, finally, forgiveness doesn't exempt anyone (including us) from facing the consequences of their actions.

So, none of what follows should be seen as denying reality or making excuses for what anyone did. We must face reality head on and not rationalize, justify, overlook or excuse what anyone did, including ourselves.

BAD DOG!

The key to experiencing forgiveness and truly letting go of any remaining emotional residue left over from the past is to understand that everyone's actions (including ours) are always a reflection of their level of consciousness or understanding. That may be a little confusing, so let's use puppies as an example.

If you get a puppy from a shelter or purchase it from a litter, what does the puppy do when you bring it home? The adorable little thing pees on your carpet and chews on your shoes, doesn't it? And while that's annoying, is the puppy being bad? Is the puppy doing something wrong or is there something wrong with the puppy itself? Of course not. You would never say, *"Spot, how could you! I can't believe you did that. Bad dog!"* To say such a thing wouldn't make any sense. The puppy is being a puppy. It's simply reflecting its level of development or maturity. The puppy is doing the only thing it knows how to do. It can't do otherwise.

Furthermore, would you take it personal? Would the puppy's behavior mean something about you? *"Spot, why are you doing this **to me**? Am I not a good enough owner? Is there something wrong with me? Does your peeing and chewing mean I'm unlovable, unworthy or flawed in some way?"* Such notions are ridiculous, right? It's not personal. The puppy's behavior has nothing to do with you.

Yes, you have to deal with the consequences—stinky carpet and ruined shoes—and that can be really frustrating (and expensive!), but it's not personal. The puppy would pee on anyone's carpet and chew on anyone's shoes. It's not about you, it's *about the puppy*. Here's the punch line:

Every human being is a puppy.

No matter how old we are, no matter how smart or spiritual we are, we're all just puppies "peeing on the carpet and chewing on shoes." In other words, we're acting our developmental age. Our words and actions are always a reflection of our level of maturity or consciousness. To expect anyone to be more mature or conscious than they are is like expecting a new puppy to scratch at the door when it wants to go out and pee. It's not possible. Everyone's actions are a reflection of their *current* level of development. We're all doing the only thing we know how to do, and it can't be otherwise.

If you've been hurt or betrayed by someone, you cannot say they should have known better any more than you could say the puppy should know better. Every single person, from members of *ISIS* to *Donald Trump* to *Pope Francis,* is acting and behaving according to their level of consciousness. Nothing else is possible.

Furthermore, whatever anyone says or does is not personal. It doesn't mean anything about you. It doesn't mean there's something wrong with you, nor does it mean that you're unlovable, not good enough or unworthy. Even if you've experienced abuse, infidelity or been deceived in some way, it's not about you. It's not personal. *It's about them.*

Yes, it hurts, and you have to feel those feelings. And yes, there may be consequences that effect your family or finances and you might have to remove someone from your life. All of that is very painful, but it's not personal.

"When you make it a strong habit not to take anything personally, you avoid many upsets in your life. Your anger, jealousy, and envy will disappear, and even your sadness will simply disappear if you don't take anything personally…Even when a situation seems so personal, even if others insult you directly, it has nothing to do with you. What they say, what they do, and the opinions they give are according to their own minds [their own puppy-ness]. Their point of view [and actions] comes from all the programming they received during domestication."

~ Don Miguel Ruiz [80]

Here's an insight that will allow you to let go of any remaining emotional residue from the past, whether you're holding on to anger and resentment toward someone else or if you're continuing to blame yourself:

It's not that we (or they) were doing the best that we could, it's that we (or they) were doing the ONLY thing that we could.

Jesus understood this. As he was being unjustly crucified, he prayed, *"Father, forgive them; for they do not know what they're doing."*[81] In other words, he recognized their "puppy-ness" and that allowed him to forgive. They weren't "villains," they weren't "wrong," for he saw that their actions were simply a reflection of their level of understanding. Therefore, how could he blame them? They were puppies, "peeing on the carpet, chewing on shoes."

Having this understanding, however, does not mean we should be doormats and allow people to hurt or harm us.[82] *ISIS* should be stopped, and we should hold people accountable for their actions and set firm boundaries.

---

[80] *The Four Agreements: A Toltec Wisdom Book,* By Don Miguel Ruiz.
[81] Luke 23:34
[82] Jesus felt that it was his mission to be crucified and thus he chose his fate.

But the bitterness we carry towards others, or the blame we direct at ourselves, all of that drops away once we see that everyone is a "puppy," doing the only thing that they know how to do.

Let's apply this.

Your past, and the relationship pain you experienced, was co-created. It was the result of your mutual childhood patterns, personality blind spots and fear-driven personas getting all mixed together forming your not-so-tasty "stew." Yet, neither of you were aware of any of that. Neither of you knew what you were doing, and therefore, how can you blame yourself or them? You were both just "puppies," reflecting your level of self-awareness at the time. Neither of you had any idea that you were contaminating the "stew" with your "ingredients." Therefore, you should pray as Jesus did (with slightly different wording), "Father, forgive *us*; for *we* didn't know what *we* were doing."

COMPASSION REPLACES CONTEMPT

When you recognize this, compassion will replace contempt for everyone in your past, including yourself.

- You'll recognize that neither of you knew how to handle your childhood pain, and that created your relationship dynamics. You'll see that it wasn't personal, and compassion will replace contempt.
- You'll recognize that neither of you knew what to do with your feelings, and that led to conflict and drama. You'll see that it wasn't personal, and compassion will replace contempt.
- You'll recognize that both of you were deeply insecure and afraid, causing you both to overcompensate by being critical or controlling. You'll see that it wasn't personal, and compassion will replace contempt.

- You'll recognize that because neither of you were truly seen as children, your selfishness was simply a survival strategy. You'll see that it wasn't personal, and compassion will replace contempt.
- You'll recognize that because you both felt empty, bored and fundamentally alone, you both left the relationship in your particular ways in an attempt to feel alive and happy. You'll see that it wasn't personal, and compassion will replace contempt.

WORKOUT!

This "workout" is a simply a "yes" or "no" answer:

- Are you willing to let go of all the anger, bitterness and resentment you've been holding on to, whether it was directed at someone else or yourself? In other words, are you willing to see that everyone was doing the *ONLY* thing they knew how to do?

— 15 —

THE PAST

&

What to Do When You're Triggered

"Let your spiritual path become the willingness to let whatever happens make it through you, rather than carrying it into the next moment."
~ Michael Singer

In the movie, *The Incredible Hulk* (2008), actor Edward Norton plays a character who is exposed to gamma radiation and the effects are profound. When his "buttons" get pushed, when he's triggered and his heartrate reaches 200 beats per minute, he transforms into *Hulk*, a very dangerous and destructive monster.[83]

Can you relate to that? I know I sure can.

As you continue on your spiritual journey, you will soon discover that as much as you think you've let go of the past, there is still quite a bit of old emotional pain stored in your body, stuff that never made it through you. This negative energy lies dormant within us until something triggers it. And like *Hulk*, when our "buttons" get pushed, look out. We, too, transform into some kind of monster. We might not do physical damage like *Hulk* does, but perhaps we become defensive, suspicious, argumentative, withdrawn, passive-aggressive, angry, closed or verbally abusive.

---

[83] If you're not familiar with the movie, here's the trailer: https://bit.ly/2te9EUE Notice he says, *"There are aspects of my personality that I cannot control. When I lose control, it's very dangerous to be around me."* The same is true of us when we're triggered.

The negative energy that is stored in our bodies is incredibly powerful and if we don't know what to do when its triggered, there's no telling the amount of damage we could do to our life and relationships. Therefore, this chapter is all about what to do when you get triggered.

THE MONSTER WITHIN

Let's begin by learning a bit more about "the monster within." Eckhart Tolle calls it the "Pain-Body," and he describes it this way in his books:

> "The remnants of pain left behind by every strong negative emotion that is not fully faced, accepted, and then let go of, join together to form an energy field that lives in the very cells of the body. It consists of not just childhood pain, but also painful emotions that were added to it later in adolescence and during your adult life...This energy field of old but still very-much-alive emotion that lives in almost every human being is the Pain-Body...Anything can trigger it, particularly if it resonates with a painful pattern from your past. When it is ready to awaken from its dormant stage, even a thought or an innocent remark can activate it."[84]

Michael Singer describes the same dynamic, only he uses the yogic (Hindu) word, "Samskara." Here's how he describes it in, *The Untethered Soul*:

> "When you are unable to allow life's events to pass through you, they stay inside and become a problem. These patterns may be held within you for a very long time...In the yogic tradition, that unfinished energy pattern is called a Samskara...A Samskara is a blockage, an impression from the past. It's an unfinished energy pattern that ends up running your life."

---

[84] The first part of the quote is from, *A New Earth,* and the last two sentences are from, *The Power of Now.*
192

Over the last couple of chapters, we've been discussing how to let go of the past and we said there are three steps involved: (1) Learning from the past, (2) Releasing any emotional residue the past has left in its wake so that we can, (3) Live and love with an open, available heart. It's this third step that we turn our attention to now.

AN OPEN, AVAILABLE HEART

Here's the reality of living in this world: *You will be triggered.* People will do and say things that open old wounds, touch soft spots and flare up old feelings. No matter how much learning and releasing you've done (steps 1 & 2 above), you will get triggered. And that is not a problem. The issue is, can you keep your heart open when you're triggered, when your "buttons" are pushed? For example, can you stay open when someone criticizes you in the same way your ex did? Or when you find out the person you're dating cheated on their partner in the past? Or when your feelings are hurt? Can you stay open in those moments? Can you stay available and present?

Again, you will get triggered. And if you close down and run away every time it happens, or if you get defensive and start an argument, or if you overreact and start interrogating someone, your love life will never be happy.

TRIGGER HAPPY

Below is a five-step process on how to keep your heart open when you're triggered. And you'll find that this process works on any type of trigger. Whether it's your mom badgering you for the hundredth time about giving her a grandchild, or your boss praising a coworker for something you did, or, as in the case I'm about to describe, when your boyfriend looks at another woman, here's how you keep your heart open so that you don't morph into your version of *Hulk*.

1. Recognize

The first step in how to handle being triggered is to *recognize* that you are, in fact, triggered. Believe it or not, this is the hardest step. So, let's use an example to illustrate the process. Consider this scenario:

> You're out to dinner with a guy you've been dating exclusively for two months (change the genders if necessary). You really like him a lot and two nights ago, you had sex for the first time. As you're having a drink and enjoying each other's company, a really gorgeous woman walks past your table and your guy turns his head and checks her out.

OK, how are you doing now? Well, you're triggered…big time. In the blink of an eye, your body-mind reacts to what you saw. Your stomach becomes queasy, your breath catches in your throat and your jaw clenches. At the same moment, the memory of your ex-husband cheating on you 18-months ago flashes before your eyes and you hear the voice in the head say, *this guy can't be trusted either.* So, in the span of two seconds, all of the anger and pain from your past comes rushing up like Old Faithful, and you're struck with an overwhelming urge to either throw your drink in his face or get up and walk out.

That's an example of the past being triggered in you. The Pain-Body is activated and your Samskaras are stimulated. But can you recognize that? Do you actually see what's happening? It's not about what your guy did. Yes, he checked her out, but he's looked at a bunch of people during dinner, including other men, and that didn't trigger you. But her, well, that triggered a bunch of old emotional pain left over from your marriage, stuff that never made it through you. And when your guy looked at her, that dormant pain got activated.

Hulk is about to appear…unless you can recognize what's happening.

Are you self-aware enough *in that moment* to simply say to yourself, "Damn, I'm triggered," and not get lost in whether or not his behavior was right or wrong? This is a huge challenge. It's very difficult to recognize that it's about you and your past, and not blame someone else for what you're experiencing.

2. Relax

If you recognize that you're triggered, that the body is reacting and the mind is racing, what do you do? Simple. Just *relax*. Don't do anything. Just sit back and watch what's happening inside of you like you'd watch children playing on a Jungle Gym. Don't get involved in the disturbance. This is hard to do because you'll notice a very strong pull to say or do something. But don't. Just relax. In a sense, lean away from the inner turbulence and keep your hands off of it. If you jump in, you'll only make it worse.

For example, imagine you're sitting beside an absolutely still pond. It's like glass, beautiful and peaceful, until a leaf falls into the water and causes some ripples. If you want the water to return to stillness, the worst thing you can do is jump in and try to smooth it out. You'll just make it worse. The same is true when you're triggered. If you do anything, you'll just make it worse.

Back to our scenario.

You see your guy looking at that gorgeous woman and you notice some "ripples on your pond" (or perhaps it's a tsunami!). The first step is to recognize that you're triggered by saying to yourself, "Damn, I'm really triggered." Then immediately do the second step, which is to relax. For a few seconds (that's all it takes) give the energy space to work itself out. Just notice what's happening in your body and mind and stay out of it.

This is being **present**. Simply be with your experience, with *what is*. There's a mess going on inside, so just be there with it. Watch it. This is called, "witness consciousness," and it's the simplest thing in the world to do—*because you're not doing anything other than paying attention.* Don't allow yourself to react. Instead, relax.

3. Release

The third step in the process is to *release* the energy that is triggered and coming up in you. And frankly, releasing is not very different from relaxing. In fact, they're like two sides of the same coin. Relaxing is about not holding on, while releasing is about letting go. One is passive, the other is active, but they're essentially the same thing.

Imagine that you're in a tug-of-war with an entire football team. It's you against them. Think of the struggle. You're holding on for dear life. But to end the struggle, all you have to do is let go of the rope. Just open your hands. And sometimes, that's all you need to do when you're triggered. Just open your hands.

Again, back to our scenario.

After seeing your guy check that woman out, your body and mind went crazy. But you recognized that by saying to yourself, "Damn, I'm triggered." Then, you relaxed by leaning away from all the inner commotion and simply observed it. Once you do those two steps—and they take only seconds— wherever your hands are, if they are literally on the table or in your lap, simply turn your palms to the sky and open your fingers. In other words, open your hands. You will not believe the freedom you will experience. It's like the energy will release right out of your fingertips.

Another releasing technique is to exhale the trapped energy right out of the body. In the 1999 movie, *The Green Mile*, the now deceased actor, Michael Clark Duncan, plays a death-row inmate who has a lot of bad stuff trapped inside of him and he releases all that negativity with a huge exhale.[85]

---

[85] Here's the scene if you're not familiar with the movie: https://bit.ly/2RPm3Z7

We can release our trigger energy that way too. Whether or not the energy is trapped in your stomach, chest or throat, use your imagination and exhale it out of your body.[86] In fact, for the deepest release, combine this practice with opening your hands.

4. Report

After you *Recognize, Relax* and *Release*, you will feel a total shift in your inner energy field (if you don't, you haven't truly done the first 3 "R's"). The inner turbulence will have calmed down, and your heart, which nearly closed in fear, will remain open and available. Even though the whole process has taken only a few seconds, it's an incredible feeling. And it's at this point that you might think the process is over. But it's not.

If you want intimacy, if you want to be close to the person who gifted you with the opportunity to face and feel some old emotional pain, then you must tell them what just happened.

However, be careful here. You're not sharing what they did **TO** you, you're sharing what happened **IN** you. In other words, you're not blaming them for your experience—they didn't have anything to do with it—you're simply reporting your experience to them. Given our scenario, it could sound something like this:

> "Hey, just a second ago, when you looked at that woman who walked by, I got really triggered by that. My stomach got queasy, my breath changed, and my jaw got really tight. It triggered all my fears and insecurities about having been cheated on in my past and I even had the thought that I shouldn't trust you. None of that is about you, of course. It's old stuff in

---

[86] You don't have to do it as dramatically as it was done in the movie. LOL! You might get put in a straight-jacket. You can do this very subtly without anyone knowing.

me that I've never let go. I just wanted you to know what happened over here when you looked at her."

In the next section of the book, we're going to talk about the relationship we have to our inner truth (which is what that was), so I won't spend a lot of time on this here. But I'm guessing that to speak to someone in the way I just described scares the crap out of you. How would they react to that kind of authentic revelation? Well, it could go any number of ways. They might feel deeply drawn to your openness (as I would be), or they might think you're a neurotic mess (which you are, we all are), or they might get triggered because you got triggered! Whatever happens from your reveal will give you an opportunity to learn and grow together.

The bottom line is this: You have to decide if you want to truly reveal yourself to someone or if you want to play games and try to control everything, including your image. More about this in the next section.

5. Repeat

The last step is easy. Repeat this process every time you recognize that you're triggered, which if you pay attention, will be dozens of times a day.

"When you're triggered, upset or hurt, be excited! Buried stuff is coming up to be released."
~ Michael Singer

WORKOUT!

Your "workout" is simple. Practice the "5 R's" every time you're triggered and then send me an email, telling me how your life has changed because of it.

— 16 —

THE PAST

&

Learning to Trust Again

"Holding on to the past is like eating a meal that made you violently sick and then asking for a doggie bag so that you can take it home and eat it again and again. 'I save all the spoiled food and taste a little bit of it every day.' That's how we deal with the past."

~ Michael Singer

We began this section of the book by saying that if we want our next relationship to be a beautiful, sustainable intimacy, we have to begin it with a clean emotional slate. That means that we have to let go of the past to such an extent that we can approach the next relationship with an open, available heart.

Just as a person who is physically fit is not carrying a lot of excess fat in their bodies, so a person who is relationally fit is not carrying a lot of excess baggage in their hearts. After you've "worked out" by learning from the past and releasing any emotional residue it left behind, the past becomes something that merely *happen-ed* not something that is *happen-ing*. You are wiser from what happened, of course, but not walled-off because of it. A truly untethered soul is one that is available not guarded, vulnerable not defended, receptive not suspicious.

Yet, the scars are real. There is no denying that our hearts were broken, and while we understand the need for a clean emotional slate, how are we ever supposed to trust again? Even if we take responsibility for our part in how the past was created, even if we release all the blame and bitterness, how are we supposed to open our hearts in trust when we're terrified that we'll just be hurt again?

Well, it depends on what we're trusting in. Yes, an untethered soul is a trusting soul, but where is that trust placed? That is the question. And there are three options, and in fact, they occur as stages in our spiritual development. Below is a description of three different stages of trust, and make no mistake about it…

What we are trusting in not only determines the degree to which our hearts will be open and available, but it also determines the amount of fear, anxiety and worry we will experience in our love lives.

STAGE 1: I trust—*YOU*.[87]

In this first stage, people make trust a function of the other person's behavior and character. This is overwhelmingly the most common perspective on trust, held by probably 95% of us. It sounds like this:

- I'll trust you if you behave in a trustworthy manner. If you don't, I won't.
- I'll trust you if your words and actions are consistently aligned. If they aren't, I won't.
- I'll trust you if you demonstrate that you care about me. If you don't, I won't.

Now, those attitudes make perfect sense to most of us because it's how trust is conventionally understood. If someone acts in trustworthy ways, we

---

[87] I learned this model and much of the perspectives shared in this chapter from Jim Dethmer, of *The Conscious Leadership Group*.

can trust them. However, there's a real problem with the *"I trust—YOU"* perspective. *People are unpredictable.* Even if someone has been trustworthy in the past, can we ever be sure of what they will or won't do in the future (I mean, didn't you think someone was trustworthy in the past? How'd that turn out?)? So, when trust is placed in a person, we can never feel truly secure. We will always experience some measure of anxiety and worry since people are, by nature, unpredictable.

But it gets worse. If trust is dependent on a person's behavior or character, you won't be able to meet a new person with an open, available heart. How could you? You don't know them yet. Therefore, during those first few crucial conversations or dates, when a meaningful connection is being explored, you'll carry an energy that says, *"I don't trust you. Not yet anyway. You have to earn it."* And nothing is more unattractive and a bigger turn-off than a guarded, suspicious heart.

Do you remember "Sally" from back in the Prologue? She was a Stage 1 person. Here's how I described it:

> "So, when Sally started dating again six months ago, she knew she had a wall around her heart, and she joked that every brick had some guys name on it. That wall was there to protect her from another loser like her husband. *Men would have to prove that they were worthy of her trust before she'd ever take down that wall.*"

Don't kid yourself. Men can feel those walls (and vice versa—it definitely goes both ways). They can feel that they're being held at arm's length because of what another guy did. And I've yet to meet a guy who's brought a sledge hammer to a date! No decent man (or woman) is interested in knocking down your walls by proving himself to you. He'll simply walk away and look for a woman who has her arms wide open. In the end, the *"I trust—YOU"* perspective will sabotage your love life and keep you single.

So, believe it or not, the goal is not to learn to trust a person. In fact, I hope your painful past has taught you never to do that again. And when you see that your trust can't be placed in a person, you're ready for Stage 2.

STAGE 2: I trust—*ME*.

The second stage, is *"I trust—ME."* This means that I trust myself to be OK regardless of what other people do or don't do. This perspective is quite rare, occurring in about 4% of people. In Stage 2, my sense of security does not come from what anybody else does "out there," it comes from what I know to be true "in here." And what I know to be true "in here" is that I am OK, and that I will be OK, regardless of what anyone says or does. I'm not trusting *them*, I'm trusting *myself*. This brings a level of inner stability that a Stage 1 person never experiences.

For example, my wife is a person of integrity. I wouldn't be with her if she wasn't. But I don't trust *her*. While I believe it's highly unlikely that she would cheat on me, she is fundamentally unpredictable. I don't know for sure what she'll do in the future (she doesn't either). But I can be at peace in the midst of such unpredictability because I know that I'll be OK no matter what she does. ***In other words, my sense of security does not come from a belief in her trustworthiness.*** No one is intrinsically trustworthy. I trust—*ME*.

This does not mean, however, that nothing can break my heart, but it does mean that nothing can break *ME*. And trusting yourself does not mean having a calloused, cynical view of people and relationships either. In fact, it has the exact opposite effect on our hearts. When our sense of security is grounded in the deep knowing that we are OK no matter what anyone does, the inner tension relaxes and our hearts open to every experience. In other words, we're finally able to be comfortable in our own skin and nothing is sexier than that.

Another important dimension of the *"I trust—ME"* perspective is that I trust myself to learn from everything and everyone that life puts in my path. Stage 2 people are so committed to curiosity and learning that they see all of life as an opportunity to learn and grow. Everything is an invitation to wake up.

"Your experience is perfect. It's just what you need. Every person, experience, condition or circumstance is exactly what you should have and what you need. So, experience it fully, go through it, learn from it, appreciate it."

~ Michael Singer

So, for example, if a person doesn't follow through on a promise (a breach of trust for a Stage 1 person), the Stage 2 person sees it as an opportunity to learn and grow. Perhaps we learn more about making clear agreements. Perhaps we learn more about taking responsibility or being candid or feeling our feelings or how to source our needs from within. Other people's actions or decisions, while potentially very painful, are seen as an opportunity for me to grow in self-awareness. And for a Stage 2 person, that's what life is all about.

Here is the motto of a Stage 2 person:

> "I trust you to be exactly who you are and to do exactly what you do. And whatever that is, I'm going to use it for my growth and learning as a person. I trust that you will always do and decide according to your level of consciousness, and that no matter what that is, I'll be OK."

Now, when people hear this, they often worry that if they trust people to be exactly who they are, that their life will be filled with people who lack integrity or they will become doormats. Neither is true.

First of all, very few people will become more trustworthy just because you badger them to do so. For the most part, people will do what they want, regardless of any pressure you put on them. Secondly, you get to choose whom to have or not have in your life. You get to surround yourself with people who keep their agreements and live a life of integrity, and you get to distance yourself from those who don't share your values, whether they are partners, friends or even family members.

The difference is that you get to live without fear, worry and anxiety. People will be exactly who they are, and no matter what that is, you know that it's not personal, that you'll be OK and that you'll even grow as a result of anything you experience. So, you can't lose, and as a result, you can live with an open, available heart, which is the most attractive way of being in the world.

Summing up, then, once you've seen that sourcing a sense of security and inner stability from another person gives you neither, and once you've learned to relax in the awareness that you'll be OK no matter what anyone does, you're ready to truly cross over and take the biggest evolutionary leap of all. You can let go of everything and simply trust LIFE.

STAGE 3: I trust—*LIFE*

Whether you call it God, The Quantum Field, Source, The Universe or any other word that describes what is beyond words, Stage 3 people trust Life.[88] But even though this stage is what all the ancient scriptures point to, only about 1% of people (at most) truly *experience* a completely untethered

---

[88] I use "Life" rather than "God" because not only is it a far less emotionally charged term, it's also the most inclusive term, for even an atheist can't deny that Life exists.

soul. Most people are still holding on to something—other people, themselves, their money, their beliefs—rather than letting go of everything and trusting Life completely.

To experience this stage is to live without fear—without the fear of rejection, without the fear of loss, without the fear of being hurt, without the fear of death, without the fear of *anything*. And this becomes possible when we choose to see Life as being "for me."

Here's how Jim Dethmer describes it in his book, *The 15 Commitments of Conscious Leadership*:

> "Einstein said that the most important question is, "Is the universe friendly?" He went on to say that if it is, then about 99% of everything we do is a waste of time because most of our lives are spent reacting to the world as though it is unfriendly. Stage 3 people understand this, not as a belief only, but as an experience in their bodies. They have fundamental trust that the universe is "for" them."

TO ME, BY ME, FOR ME

Stage 1 people have a "to me," *victim* mindset, meaning, their ability to trust and feel secure is based on, *or is at the effect of*, the other person's character and behavior. Stage 2 people, conversely, have a "by me," *creator* mindset, meaning, their ability to trust and feel secure comes from within themselves. It's not dependent on what anyone else says or does. They trust themselves to be OK and learn from everything that occurs.

Stage 3 people have a "for me," *surrender* mindset. They see the universe as being inherently friendly, and therefore, they simply surrender into what A.H. Almaas calls, "Basic Trust."

> *Basic Trust* is a non-conceptual, implicit trust or confidence that whatever is optimal will happen, the sense that no matter what happens, all is well and will be well. It is the confidence that

reality is ultimately good; that nature, the universe, and all that exists is "for you," that its very nature is trustworthy…If *Basic Trust* informs your experience, your psyche is relaxed. Your soul is at peace with itself, your situation, even your relationship status. You rest in the unquestioned confidence that the universe provides, that you have and will receive what you really need, and that things are workable.[89]

Imagine the difference this kind of "basic trust" would have on your life! Wouldn't the "for me" mindset change your perspective on your past? And wouldn't the "for me" mindset free you from any worry about a future relationship and what might happen? Wouldn't your heart be wide open and available? Of course it would.

People who trust that the Universe is "for me" have come to this knowing through devoted practice. It doesn't happen by magic. It's usually the result of many years of meditation, inquiry and spiritual work.[90] The spiritual path is about evolving through the stages of seeing Life as happening "to me," then "by me," and ultimately, "for me."

"You are sitting on a rock spinning around in empty space in the middle of absolutely nowhere. This has been going on for billions of years and you'll be here for about 80. Given that, what did you say you're worried about?"
~ Michael Singer

---

[89] A.H. Almaas, *Facets of Unity: The Enneagram of Holy Ideas*. You may remember that I shared a part of this quote in Chapter 5, and it's so powerful, it bears repeating.
[90] The best way to move beyond the "to me" mindset and develop the "by me" or even "for me" mindset is to join one of my *Online Relationship Bootcamps*. For information visit, www.coachingwithroy.com. Also, Appendix I describes a number of resources that will support this kind of growth in your life.

WORKOUT!

We've spoken enough about the past. Let's focus on the future. If you were to truly embody either the "by me" or "for me" mindsets, how would that specifically show up in the way you date and relate? What would you do or say differently? What attitude or fear would change? In other words, write a paragraph in your journal describing what you would look like if you had a truly open and available heart?

WORKOUT #5

STRENGTHENING YOUR RELATIONSHIP TO YOUR TRUTH

CONCEAL or REVEAL

Chapter 17: Truth & The Games People Play

Chapter 18: Truth & Choosing Your Love Language

Chapter 19: Truth & How to Speak Unarguably

"When you're not seeking someone's love, acceptance or approval, you can afford to tell the truth of this moment, which is the truth of who you are. There's no risk. You start to see that the real risk is in not telling the truth— you risk living a life of inauthenticity, of held-back-ness, of disconnection and quiet desperation. You live as an image, and you feel distant from the one you love or the one you seek to love."

~ Jeff Foster

— 17 —

TRUTH

&

The Games People Play

"If you search for tenderness, it isn't hard to find;
you can have the love you need to live.
But if you look for truthfulness, you might just as well be blind;
it always seems to be so hard to give.
Honesty is such a lonely word, everyone is so untrue;
Honesty is hardly ever heard, and mostly what I need from you."
~ Billy Joel [91]

Let's begin with a question.

Would you rather be in a relationship where people play games, or would you rather be in one where people are open, honest and authentic?

I often ask that question when I'm giving a talk or working with clients, and it probably wouldn't surprise you to know that I have never once had a person say that they wanted a relationship where people played games. No one wants secrets, withholds, half-truths or outright lies. And no one wants to be a person or date a person who is insincere, manipulative or fake. No one wants that...until they hear what it means to be truly authentic. Then it's often a very different story.

---

[91] If you're not familiar with this beautiful and powerful song, here it is: https://bit.ly/1rd2uex

In this section of the book, we're going to strengthen your relationship to your truth. And notice I didn't say *the* truth. When I talk about truth, I'm not talking about what you believe about God, science, history, politics or even spirituality. No, I'm talking about your truth, what's going on inside of you, *your inner reality.* I'm talking about your thoughts, feelings, body sensations, wants, wonderings and worries.

I want to know what you do with that.

Do you reveal it, or do you conceal it? Those are the only two options. In any moment, you can either reveal what's true for you and about you, or you can conceal your inner reality in an attempt to control how you're perceived. It's that black and white. You're either "showing your cards" and making yourself known, or, out of fear, you're "holding them close to the chest" and playing some sort of game. In other words, you're either revealing or concealing.

"Taking the easy way out or telling the truth—these are not merely two different choices. They are different pathways through life. They are utterly different ways of existing."
~ Jordan B. Peterson [92]

This "workout" is going to challenge you to be a revealer rather than a concealer. And of all the inner relationships we're exploring in this book, this one is unquestionably the easiest to understand—just be honest about your experience—*but it is, by far, the most terrifying to practice.* What if they don't like what we reveal? What if they, in fact, judge and reject us? For example…

---

[92] *12 Rules for Life*, by Jordan B. Peterson. He's a very polarizing guy, but his book has some great things to say about honesty.

212

- What if they knew that I'm needy and lonely?

- What if they knew that I'm insecure and jealous?

- What if they knew that I'm self-conscious about my body and worried that I won't be able to satisfy them sexually?

- What if they knew that I'm so suspicious and untrusting that I've done a thorough background search on them?

- What if they knew that I don't believe in God?

- What if they knew my divorce isn't final yet and that it's really contentious and filled with drama?

- What if they knew I lost my job and I'm living with my parents?

- What if they knew I think they might be a player?

- What if they knew that I wanted to know how much money they make and that it would make a difference to me?

- What if they knew I had an affair when I was married?

- What if they knew that even though it's our first date, I'm already thinking they're "the one" and wondering how beautiful our children would be?

———————————

"The question to always ask yourself is this: what is my truth in this moment? In other words, what do I really think and feel right now? Can I simply admit what is appearing in present experience? Can I begin to admit these thoughts, these sensations, these feelings, however much I don't want to admit them, however much they threaten my image of myself?"
~ Jeff Foster [93]

———————————

[93] *The Deepest Acceptance: Radical Awakening in Ordinary Life*, by Jeff Foster. All of his quotes are from this great book.

It's one thing to let someone know what kind of music you like or what your favorite football team is, but what if they knew our *inner* truth, the things we may not even want to admit to ourselves? What if they knew things like that?

All of us want an open, honest and authentic relationship—in *theory*. But in *reality*—because we are so afraid of being judged and rejected—we play games. It's just too risky to reveal our inner truth and make ourselves known. So instead, we conceal, choosing only to show the parts of us that we feel others will find attractive and desirable. The truth is…

We fear that if we were known, we'd be alone.

WHAT IS INTIMACY?

Since this book is about the pursuit of intimacy, let's define it. The simplest and most accurate definition of intimacy is "knowing and being known." It's when two people, whether they are friends, relatives or lovers, truly see each other. It's when nothing is concealed or hidden. Intimacy is being exposed, revealed and seen. It is, in fact, being "naked."

Humanity's first mythical couple, Adam and Eve, are a beautiful picture of this. They were in paradise and here's how their relationship was described:

> "For this reason, a man shall leave his father and his mother, and cleave to his wife; and the two shall become one flesh. *And the man and his wife were both naked and unashamed.* "[94]

Please don't take their nakedness literally as if they hadn't yet gone to "Paradise Mall" and bought some *Calvin Klein's*. It means they were emotionally naked before one another. Nothing was concealed, hidden or

---

[94] Genesis 2:24-25

covered up. You could say they were "laid bare" and "stripped" of any pretense. In other words, there were no secrets between them. Everything was revealed, exposed and seen.

And neither of them had any shame or judgment about themselves or each other. What they were showing and seeing was met with complete acceptance and unconditional love. They were standing before each other saying, *"Here I am. This is me, warts and all."* And in response, they said to each other, *"I see you. I see everything about you…and I love you."*

That is paradise.

That is intimacy.

And only fear stands in the way of our experiencing it.

LET'S GET NAKED!

The only way we will ever experience authentic intimacy is if we "get naked" and stop hiding, pretending and playing games. That means pushing through the fear and choosing to reveal ourselves to another person.

Could they judge and reject us? Yes, of course. There will always be people who can't handle our inner truth. Will their rejection hurt? Sure. But what's the alternative? Playing games and settling for superficial, fake relationships? Aren't you sick of that? Haven't you had enough of those kinds of relationships? Are you ready to take what will be, perhaps, the biggest risk of your life? Are you ready to reveal and not a conceal?

Are you ready to risk being judged and rejected in exchange for the opportunity to experience authentic—*naked and unashamed*—intimacy?

Well, maybe not. At least not yet, and I respect that.

I realize that what I'm suggesting is outrageous. In fact, I doubt that there's a single person in your life that would support you in living and loving in the way I'm suggesting. Even most relationship professionals would never suggest (as I do) that you reveal the kinds of things I described in the bullet points above. *They will tell you how to play the game better while I'm challenging you to quit playing the game altogether.* The path to authentic intimacy happens only if we're willing to reveal and make our inner truth known. So, again, I recognize the enormity of what I'm suggesting. I'm inviting you to completely change your way of relating. But here is something that I've learned:

The costs of concealing far outweigh the risks of revealing.

In fact, the costs of concealing are more like guaranteed outcomes. As long as you "keep your clothes on" and conceal your inner truth, you're guaranteed to experience the following 5 things.

1. You are guaranteed to have the honeymoon end.

As I mentioned a moment ago, when you withhold your inner truth, you are only showing the parts of you that you believe someone will find attractive or desirable. But that means they never fall in love with the real you, but only with the image you've presented. Consequently, you have to work very hard at keeping the other person from ever seeing the real you, and that's not only exhausting, it is destined to fail. You will slip up. Eventually they will see you "naked" and the honeymoon will be over. *"Who are you?"* they will say. *"You aren't the person I fell in love with."* And the sad thing is, they'll be right.

"In the early stages of many so-called romantic relationships, role-playing is quite common in order to attract and keep whoever is perceived by the ego as the one who is going to 'make me happy, make me feel special, and fulfill all my needs.' 'I'll play who you want me to be, and you'll play who I want you to be.' That's the unspoken and unconscious agreement. However, role-playing is hard work, and so those roles cannot be sustained indefinitely, especially once you start living together."

~ Eckhart Tolle

2. You are guaranteed to never feel truly secure.

What you most deeply want is to be loved for who you are. But when you withhold your inner truth, when you play games by concealing your thoughts, feelings, judgments and worries, you never get to feel truly loved for who you are because you're not showing them who you are. In the back of your mind, you'll always have a thought that says, *if they really knew me, they wouldn't love me.* Consequently, you live with the fear of being found out, and you never get to feel truly safe and secure in someone's love.

3. You are guaranteed to have the Law of Attraction work against you.

The Law of Attraction basically means "like attracts like." And even though I take issue with the LOA (see Chapter 6), that doesn't mean there isn't some truth to it. Like *does* attract like, and in this context that means if you're playing games, you'll attract someone who plays games, too.

For example, if you go to a soccer field with a soccer ball, you will attract people who want to play soccer. You won't attract people who want to play basketball. That's a different game. The same is true in your love life. If your "game" is revealing, you will attract people who want to reveal. But if your "game" is concealing, you'll attract people who want to conceal. **You**

will always and *only* attract people (intimately or otherwise) who are committed to playing the same game that you're playing.

This is both good and bad news. The bad news is that if you tend to attract people that play games, that means you must be playing games. It can't be otherwise. But the good news is that if you want to attract someone who doesn't play games, someone who is committed to candor and authenticity, then all you have to do is live that way yourself and the Law of Attraction will work for you and not against you.

4. You are guaranteed to be lonely.

Loneliness is horrible. To feel separate, disconnected and alone is just about the worst feeling in life. *Yet the true cause of loneliness is misunderstood.* It's not the result of being single or not having an active social life. It's got nothing to do with that. **Loneliness is a self-inflicted condition. It's caused by concealing.** If you won't let anyone truly see you, if you're hiding and pretending, you'll always feel lonely even if you're surrounded by people. However, if you choose to reveal and run around "naked" in this world, trust me, you won't be lonely.

"If I calculate and put on phony behavior in order to please you…I cannot really receive your love. It is poisoned by my knowledge that the love is for the image I have created, not for me. Since I have shut myself off from your love in this way, I will feel more lonely and unloved, and try even more desperately to manipulate myself and you in order to get this love."
~ Brad Blanton [95]

---

[95] *Radical Honesty: How to Transform Your Life by Telling the Truth*, by Brad Blanton.

5. You are guaranteed to deplete your energy.

Perhaps the most significant result of concealing is a loss of energy and aliveness. When we withhold, hide or pretend, our life-force is weakened or depleted. In other words, playing games affects the way we feel. It kinks our "hose" and our energy can't flow. We will explore the flow of our life-force more fully in Section 6, but for now, Jim Dethmer describes it this way:

> "For the individual who withholds, the major problem is a decrease in energy…When we withhold, this energy flow is dampened, or in some cases, blocked altogether. From our perspective, withholding is not a moral issue (Thou shalt not lie and withhold because it is wrong!), but rather an energetic one. When we withhold, we cut ourselves off from the free flow of energy that is necessary for individual and collective creativity."

In my view, those 5 *guaranteed* outcomes are far worse than being judged and rejected by a few people who are terrified to engage authentically and would rather play games. Do you agree? Isn't revealing worth the risk?

WORKOUT!

Record your answers to the following questions in your journal. Be sure to include any thoughts, feelings or body sensations that arise.

1. Are you willing to risk being judged and rejected in exchange for the opportunity to experience authentic—*naked and unashamed*—intimacy?
2. If you said, "yes," from whom have you been concealing? A friend, relative, lover, co-worker, etc.? Who have you been playing games with?

3. For those you just identified, if you're willing to "get naked," go to those people and share with them your answers to the following statements:

      - If you really knew me, you'd know that...
      - I'm afraid you'd judge me if you knew...
      - A feeling I haven't expressed is...
      - One of the ways I have been pretending is...
      - A lie I've told you is...

4. When are you going to do this?

— 18 —

TRUTH

&

Choosing Your Love Language

"There are two basic motivating forces: fear and love. When we are afraid, we pull back from life. When we are in love, we open to all that life has to offer with passion, excitement, and acceptance."

~ John Lennon [96]

What's your favorite sitcom? For many, it's shows like *Friends*, *Seinfeld* or *The Office*. If you're really "old school," perhaps it's *I Love Lucy* or *The Andy Griffith Show*. My favorite is definitely *The Big Bang Theory*. I absolutely love that show. I think I've seen every episode at least once.

The reason I bring this up is because I think a lot of people, single or otherwise, feel like they're living in a sitcom—*except it's not so funny*. For most people, the pursuit of intimacy is not a "situation comedy," it's more like a "situation confusing." In other words, the situations we find ourselves in are better described as "OMG!" than "LOL."

For example, here are a few "situations" that my clients have asked my advice about recently. You'll notice they aren't very funny.

---

[96] I have no idea where this quote came from, though my research shows it's accurate. To my knowledge, it's not from any of the songs he wrote.

- "Roy, I've been on a couple dates with a guy I really like, but both times he's drank a lot. I'm really uncomfortable with it. How do I handle that?"

- "Roy, I've been out with this guy twice and I really like him. But he wants us to take our profiles down and see each other exclusively, and I'm not ready for that yet. What should I say to him?"

- "Roy, because of my divorce and a recent job change, I'm financially strapped. But I've just met someone, and I'd like to take her to nice places and do things with her, but I just can't afford it right now. How do I tell her that?"

- "Roy, I met this guy and we have incredible chemistry, but since I've been burned in the past by having sex too soon, I want to wait for at least a couple of months. How should I handle this?"

- Roy, my best friend is setting me up with one of his wife's girlfriends and I'm really looking forward to meeting her. But even though my marriage is long over, the divorce isn't final yet and it's really ugly and contentious. My kids are having a really hard time, too. In other words, my life is a mess. What do I tell her?"

THE REAL QUESTION

There's nothing funny about these types of situations or any of a hundred other situations I could have described. They are real-life, and people are genuinely confused and at a loss as to how to handle such situations. So, they ask me what to do or say.

And I never answer.

In fact, not only do I not answer their questions, I usually turn it around and ask a question of my own. I ask, *"What are you really asking me?"* This often confuses the person. "What do you mean, what am I really asking you? Isn't it obvious? I want to know how to tell someone (see the bullet points) that I'm concerned about their drinking, or that I'm not ready to be exclusive, or that I'm broke, or that I'm not ready for sex, or that my life is a mess."

And my answer is always the same:

> "That's not what you're asking me. You want to know how to control the other person's response. You're asking me how to control the outcome. Don't kid yourself. You know what to say. You just said it to me! You beautifully articulated your thoughts, feelings, wants and worries. So, you know exactly what to say. What you want to know is how to say it in a way that allows you to control the situation. That's the real question you're asking."

This is a critical point to understand about communication. We can't play the victim by saying, "I don't know what to say." Of course we know what to say. We're just afraid of what might happen if we say it.

As an example, let's go back and look at just the first bullet point. The scenario was that you're out with someone you really like but you're uncomfortable with how much they drink. I was asked, "Roy, how do I handle that?" Well, it's easy. Just say, "I really like you, but I'm uncomfortable with how much you drink. I'm scaring myself because I'm making up a story that you might have a drinking problem and I'm unwilling to be in a relationship with someone like that."

Every word of that is your inner truth. So, why not look him in the eye and just say it? Well, it's obvious. You like him and you're afraid if you "get naked" like that, he'll think you're controlling and judgmental and you'll never see him again.

"To be honest means to tell the truth without expectation, without aiming for a particular result. Honesty means telling the truth and being willing to experience everything that follows."

~ Jeff Foster

It's the same thing for every one of those bullet points (or any other situation you can imagine). Just speak your inner truth: "I'm not ready to be exclusive, and I'm afraid you won't want to keep seeing me because of that," or "I don't have the money to take you to nice places, and I'm worried you'll think I'm a loser," and so on. Just "live out loud."[97] What could be easier? But we don't because we're afraid of what might happen if we do. This is a critical issue because…

You will never have a deeply satisfying and sustainable relationship (intimate or otherwise) if fear is your real love language.

THE REAL LOVE LANGUAGES

Many years ago, I was sitting in a *Starbucks* with my friend, Jim Dethmer. We were discussing spiritual matters, as we usually do, and on this particular occasion, the topic was communication. At the time, my love life was an absolute mess and it was largely because I had a serious lack of self-awareness about what was truly motivating me in relationships. So, in an effort to open my eyes, Jim grabbed a napkin and sketched out a diagram (below) that helped me understand the two underlying forces that govern the way we relate and communicate, not only with intimate partners, but with anyone.

---

[97] By now, you have probably come up with a few questions or objections about the idea of revealing. Hold those thoughts, because at the end of the next chapter, I cover a number of the most common objections people have to revealing. And if I don't address yours, please feel free to email me (coachingwithroy@gmail.com).

224

What I learned that day was that communication is motivated by either *Fear* or *Trust*. Those are the two forces that govern or determine what comes out of our mouths, moment to moment. In a sense, then, we can think of these two motivations as our real "love languages."[98] We're either speaking in "Fear-ese," or "Trust-ese." Let's take a closer look.

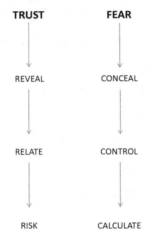

THE REAL LOVE LANGUAGES
The True Motives that Govern What We Say

TRUST	FEAR
↓	↓
REVEAL	CONCEAL
↓	↓
RELATE	CONTROL
↓	↓
RISK	CALCULATE

FEAR

When we're coming from fear, when we're speaking in that "love language," we *conceal*. Like a turtle that withdraws and hides its head when it's scared, so we withdraw and hide when we're scared. We can do this by outright lying, of course, but more than likely it shows up in the form of withholding or concealing our inner truth. And we do that to avoid a negative result, be it ridicule, rejection or retaliation.

But if you look very closely, you'll see that we conceal in order to *control*. The reason we hide, present an image or withhold our inner truth is

---

[98] Gary Chapman made the idea of "love languages" popular in his book, *The Five Love Languages*. While I am not a fan of his work (in my view, his philosophy encourages co-dependence) the phrase, "love languages," is catchy and quite useful in this context. For a formal evaluation and critique of Chapman's philosophy, see my blog: https://bit.ly/1CvzpR1

to control the relationship and avoid some sort of perceived negative outcome. We saw that in the situations I presented above. *My clients were not asking me what to say, but how to control the other person's response.* Do you see that you do the same thing—All. The. Time.? Are you brave enough to admit that you're a control freak? It's actually a critical step in your spiritual journey to recognize this. You are constantly trying to control everything, and that's quite a challenge.

Therefore, you have to spend a lot of energy and effort **calculating** what to say, how to say it, when to say it, if you should say it at all, and what will happen if you do say it or what might happen if you don't. It's exhausting, but that's the game you're forced to play if fear is your "love language."

You can't ever let your guard down and just be real. You can never simply relax and be authentic, because you're too scared about what might happen if you were to reveal your inner truth. Therefore, you have to figure out who you need to be and what you need to say (or not say) in order to control the situation. As a result, you end up imagining various scenarios in your head, calculating the possible outcomes:

- "If I tell them what I'm thinking, they'll think I'm crazy and probably walk away."
- "If I revealed my feelings, they would think I'm needy and desperate, and I'd probably never hear from them again."
- "If I were to actually say what I wanted, they would think I'm selfish and reject me."
- "If I told them that what they said hurt my feelings, they'd think I was overly sensitive and high-maintenance and they'd be turned off."
- "If I said I felt angry because they were late, I'd offend them, and this would probably be our last date."

Talk about OMG! That is so much work.

But what if you decided fear was not going to run your life, and instead, chose *trust* as the force that governs the way you relate and communicate? What would happen then? Well, let's take a look at this other "love language," one that we all know how to speak, but rarely do.

TRUST

To be governed or motivated by trust means that you're coming from the highest or deepest part of your being. It means that you're relating and communicating from the part of you that feels safe, whole and complete. It's the part of you that feels imperturbable and unafraid of being judged or rejected. It's the place in you that feels the oneness of Life and knows that you are rooted and sourced and secure in the Ground of Being.

Believe it or not, that place does exist in you. It's always there, just on the other side of the fear. And when you're coming from that place, you naturally and fearlessly *reveal*. Why wouldn't you? You have nothing to lose! Because you are whole and complete unto yourself, you don't need someone's love and acceptance, *you already are loved and accepted.* Therefore, you're totally free to "get naked" and be real.

You'd be like a billionaire playing the lottery.

If you were wildly rich, you wouldn't play the lottery because you need an outcome. You'd buy a ticket only because it's fun to play and you want to see what happens. Likewise, when you recognize that spiritually you're a billionaire, you don't seek a specific outcome. There's no need to get someone to love and accept you because you already are. From this awareness, you relate and communicate truthfully because it's fun to "buy a ticket and see what happens."

Conversely, when you're coming from fear, it's like you're buying a lottery ticket with your very last dollar. Now it matters. Now something is as stake. Now you have to win, and you'll attempt to manipulate and control everything to do so. But you can opt out of that exhausting nightmare right now. You can reveal in order to *relate*.

Notice you aren't actually relating when you're coming from fear. In order to experience a true relationship, you have to be real. You can't be pretending. To do so is playing games, and when you're doing that, they aren't relating with you, but with the image you're presenting. And I don't know what that is, but it's not a relationship. No matter how "close" you become, it will always feel hollow and unsatisfying.

"I can't think of any situation where total honesty is not going to bring about a more authentic, more real relationship. Even if that honesty results in changes that are uncomfortable at first…being honest…can never be wrong."
~ Jeff Foster

Now, I know what you're thinking. If you come from trust and choose to reveal in order to relate, you're taking a big *risk*. And that's true, you are. If you "live out loud," revealing your inner truth and making yourself known, you are choosing to let go of control and you don't know what will happen. You will wonder, *If I "get naked," will they love and accept what they see?* Maybe, maybe not. But if you're coming from trust, that doesn't matter. Like I mentioned in Chapter 16, trust means that no matter what happens, you know you'll be OK, that Life is unfolding "for you." Trust means that you have an unquestioned confidence that the universe provides and that you have and will receive what you really need. From that awareness, you let go and you embark on the most amazing adventure of your life.

You choose to *reveal* in order to *relate* and it's worth the *risk*, because in reality, you have nothing to lose and only a real relationship to gain.

Are you willing to learn a new language? Are you willing to speak "trust-ese" and quit using your native language, "fear-ese"? The process begins by setting the intention to do so. Do you want to live like this? Do you want to be a revealer and not a concealer? Once that decision is made, you practice revealing as best you can, on a moment-to-moment basis. You *will* fall back into your old habits of concealing, controlling and calculating, and when you do, simply shift back and reveal in order to relate, realizing there really isn't anything to lose, but everything to gain.

WORKOUT!

This section of the book is about strengthening your relationship to your inner truth by choosing to reveal rather than conceal. Well, your "concealing muscle" is probably very strong—it's been used a lot—while your "revealing muscle" is probably really weak. Therefore, you might not have the "strength" to reveal in a dating or relating situation—yet. Even if you intend to do so, it might be a little much at this point in your journey.

So, I want to give you a very easy "workout" to begin strengthening your "revealing muscle." It's called a ***Check-In*** and it's best done with a friend who's also interested in living consciously (but you can do it alone). Every day, whether it's in person or over the phone, each of you take turns completing the following sentences:

1. "The sensation I'm experiencing in my body right now is…"
2. "The emotion that I'm currently experiencing is…"
3. "The thought I'm having in this moment is…"
4. "The desire that I'm most aware of right now is…"

The answers to those four questions describe your inner truth. And by answering them regularly, with a friend or on your own, you're strengthening your "revealing muscle," and that prepares you to master the most important communication technique of all: the ability to speak unarguably. And we turn our attention to that now.

— 19 —

TRUTH

&

Learning to Speak Unarguably

"Communication is as simple as putting the present moment into words."
~ Jeff Foster

Tammy, a former client of mine, had been dating Phil for a couple of months and things were going great.[99] She was crazy about him and from what I could tell, he was crazy about her too. But she was withholding from him, and she knew that if she didn't "get naked" and reveal her inner truth, this relationship would fall apart like all her other relationships had.

The backstory was that Tammy had hired a headhunter to help her find a new job. She told Phil about that, of course, but what she left out was that she had previously dated the guy for about a year. While that was a long time ago and she didn't have any romantic interest in him, Tammy did respect him professionally, and since they knew each other so well, she thought he was an ideal person to help with her job search.

Tammy knew, however, that if she wanted to truly relate with Phil and not play games, she would need to take the risk of revealing *everything* to him. They were in the kitchen together and here's how that conversation went:

---

[99] Not their real names.

Tammy: *There's something I haven't told you about my headhunter and it's really bothering me. In past relationships, I often withheld things that I thought might upset my partner, but I want us to be truly honest with each other and I haven't been.*

Phil: *Ok, what is it?*

Tammy: *A number of years ago, I dated him. We were together for about a year. I don't have any romantic interest in him whatsoever, but he's good at his job and I thought he might be able to help me.*

Phil: *What?! That's bullshit! There are plenty of headhunters in the world. Why would you choose someone you slept with? You know he wants to fuck you, and you get off on male attention. Don't give me some bullshit that you're just friends. It's more than that and you know it!*

Tammy: *He doesn't want to have sex and we are just friends. I can't believe you're so jealous! There's nothing going on. And who are you to talk anyway? You go to bars with your buddies all the time and I know how many women "friends" you have. I've seen how they look at you and I've seen you flirt with them. If anyone needs attention, it's you, not me.*

Phil: *I'm not jealous and don't you dare turn this around and make it be about me. This is about you and how naïve and needy you are. He wants you and I think you know it, and you get off on it. I can't trust you because one man will never be enough for you. You'll always need some other guy hitting on you.*

Tammy: *I knew I shouldn't have told you. You're so insecure and jealous. Why do I even bother?* [At this point she storms out and locks herself in the bedroom.]

Well, that got out of hand in a hurry, didn't it? And I'm guessing you're surprised by that. When Tammy chose to reveal rather than conceal, you probably expected a beautiful moment to occur between them, didn't you? But, in fact, the opposite happened. So, perhaps their interaction leaves you scratching your head wondering—does honesty and openness, in fact, lead to drama and conflict, as I've suspected all along?

Yes, it does…if you don't know how to speak unarguably.

LEARNING HOW TO TALK

In the final chapter of this section, I'm going to teach you how to talk. Does that sound silly? On the surface it might, but actually, it's not. Like Tammy and Phil, most of us are quite good at speaking in a way that creates drama and discord, but very few of us know how to communicate in a way that creates connection and communion. And to do that, we need to learn the skill of speaking unarguably.

And it is a skill. Make no mistake about it. Speaking unarguably is not a gift, a talent or some sort of special ability you're born with. Like playing the piano, this is something you have to learn how to do. But once you master this skill, you'll be able to end drama and connect authentically with people in ways you've never thought possible.

Before I circle back to Tammy and Phil's situation and show you what could have happened if they chose to speak unarguably, I need to explain what speaking unarguably means, because it's sort of a weird phrase.

A PROFOUND IMPLICATION

Speaking unarguably means saying things that no one could argue or disagree with. It's as simple as that, but it carries a profound implication. If you don't say anything that anyone could argue with, do you see that you would never have an argument? By definition, it would be impossible. The only way to have an argument is by saying something others could argue with. Now, of course, they might not *like* what you're saying, but if what you're saying is unarguable, they can't argue with it, and therefore, it won't create drama.

Consequently, you can immediately stop any argument—or prevent one from ever happening in the first place—by never saying anything anyone could argue or disagree with. And if you master this skill, you can go the rest of your life without ever experiencing drama again.

WHAT'S UNARGUABLE?

There's a catch, of course. And the catch is that there are very, very few things that are truly unarguable. *In fact, the only things that are unarguable are your thoughts, body sensations, feelings and wants.* That's it.[100] Therefore, speaking unarguably means revealing, or reporting, on those four things. In other words, if you only talk about those four things, you will never experience drama or conflict. Let's briefly explore them.

Thoughts—The first thing that is unarguable is what you're thinking about (including things you're picturing, imagining or remembering). If you say, "I'm having the thought that a chocolate shake from *Dairy Queen* would taste amazing right now," who could argue with that? That is what you're thinking, isn't it? Therefore, it's unarguable.

Here's another example. If you say to your partner, "I'm having the thought that you don't love me anymore," that might not be *true*—they might, in fact, still love you—but what's unarguable is that you're having that thought. Do you see the distinction? There's a big difference between *having* a thought and being *right* about it.

Speaking Unarguably is not about being *right*, it's about being *real*.

---

[100] Facts are unarguable, too. And a fact is either a scientific or mathematical reality, like gravity or two-plus-two equaling four, but it's also anything a video camera could record.

We all have opinions, judgments, stories, beliefs, likes and dislikes. That's not a problem. They don't cause drama, conflict or arguments in and of themselves. *What causes drama is wanting to be right about them.* Drama happens when we confuse our stories, opinions or beliefs for *facts* or Truth (with a capital "T"). When we are "right," that means others then are "wrong," and that's what causes drama and conflict.

This is what happened with Tammy and Phil. Initially Tammy did great. She spoke unarguably by revealing what she had withheld from Phil. But after that, it quickly spiraled into drama because neither of them chose to talk about what was happening inside of them. Instead, they both wanted to be *right* about who was the real attention addict, and predictably, it turned into a full-blown fight.

Body Sensations—The second thing that is unarguable are the physical sensations occurring in your body. For example, if you said, "When I hear that you think I don't love you anymore, I notice a heaviness in my chest and I'm finding it hard to breathe," can your partner argue with that? Of course not. It's unarguable.

Feelings—The third thing that is unarguable are the feelings or emotions that you are experiencing in any given moment. Let's go back to our example. "When I hear that you think I don't love you anymore, I notice a heaviness in my chest and I'm finding it hard to breathe. I feel really sad." Can anyone disagree with that?

Wants—The final thing that is unarguable are our wants. We all have desires, needs, wishes and wants. We may or may not be able to get what we want, but it's unarguable that we want it. Again, here's how it might look in our example: "When I hear that you think I don't love you anymore, I notice a heaviness in my chest and I'm finding it hard to breathe. I feel really sad and I want to know what I'm doing that's making you feel that way."

Believe it or not, if you commit to speaking unarguably by revealing your thoughts, body sensations, feelings and wants, not only will you end drama, but you'll experience a level of aliveness, clarity and authenticity that you never imagined possible.

"Instead of habitual, automatic reactions, our words can become conscious responses based firmly on the awareness of what we are perceiving, feeling and wanting. We are led to express ourselves, then, with honesty and clarity."
~ Marshall B. Rosenberg [101]

TAMMY & PHIL—2.0

Let's return to Tammy and Phil, only this time, let's imagine that they have both learned to speak unarguably. Here's how the conversation in the kitchen could have went:

Tammy: *There's something I haven't told you about my headhunter and it's really bothering me. In past relationships, I often withheld things that I thought might upset my partner, but I want us to be truly honest with each other and I haven't been.*

Phil: *Ok. I notice my stomach just tightened up and I feel scared. [Phil takes a second to be with his experience by putting his hand on his stomach and breathing into the tightness.]*

Tammy: *I notice a tingling sensation all over my body when I see you honor your experience like that.* [Tammy notices Phil

---

[101] *Nonviolent Communication*, by Marshall B. Rosenberg. Another great book.

236

seems ready to receive what she has to say and continues.] *Phil, a number of years ago, I dated my headhunter. We were together for about a year. I don't have any romantic interest in him whatsoever, but he's good at his job and I thought he might be able to help me.*

Phil: [After taking a moment to breathe and check in with himself, Phil responds] *Wow, I'm triggered. I can feel heat in my shoulders and neck. I feel really angry that you've withheld that from me.* [Phil shrugs his shoulders a number of times and rolls his head around in circles. Then he takes a deep breath and lets out a very loud angry scream. Once he feels his anger release, he continues.] *I'm making up the story that you still have feelings for him and that I'm not enough for you. I feel a heavy pressure in my chest as I say that, and I'm really scared about our relationship.*

Tammy: [She places her hands on her heart as her eyes fill with tears.] *Phil, I feel so sad right now. I take complete responsibility for withholding from you and I totally understand your anger and your thought that I have feelings for him. Truthfully, though, I don't. But what is true is that I thought you'd get jealous and perhaps even leave me if you knew I wanted to reach out to an old boyfriend for career advice. I see that I was trying to control you, your reaction and possibly the future of our relationship by withholding from you. I am committed to not doing that anymore.*

Phil: *Well, what's true about me is that I can be jealous and insecure, and you've seen that in me before, so I take responsibility for creating an environment where you might be afraid to be honest with me. And I feel an openness in my chest right now in admitting that. Tammy, there's something I want; actually, it's more of a request. Would you be willing to fill me in on everything you're doing and talking about with your headhunter, including any romantic feelings or exchanges that might occur?*

Tammy: *Yes, absolutely. And know that you are enough for me.* [At this point, she grabs Phil's hand and takes him to the bedroom.]

So, which interaction would you prefer? Well, if you master the skill of speaking unarguably, if you commit to revealing your thoughts, sensations, feelings and wants—especially during intense moments and important conversations—then you, too, can experience the wonder of authentic intimacy.[102]

QUESTIONS & ANSWERS

Whenever honesty and openness are discussed, a number of questions and objections arise. So, before we move on the next section of the book, I'd like to address three of the most common ones.

Question #1: *"Roy, what if speaking my inner truth would hurt someone's feelings? Wouldn't it be better to conceal in that situation?"*

---

[102] If you feel that you might need some training on how to communicate like this, you'd be right and you're not alone. We all need training on how to speak unarguably. That's why you should consider working privately with me or joining one of my *Online Relationship Bootcamps*. So, as I've said repeatedly, for information on either of those options, visit www.coachingwithroy.com or email me at coachingwithroy@gmail.com.

Answer: No, but this is a very common concern. First of all, remember that when you speak unarguably, *you're speaking about yourself,* not the other person. There's no blaming, criticizing, labeling, judging, name-calling or making someone wrong, and without that, it's pretty hard to hurt someone's feelings.

However, revealing your inner truth can trigger people and hurt feelings can happen. For example, if you tell someone that you're not attracted to them or if you tell your mom that you feel very angry when she bugs you about giving her a grandchild, or if you tell your best friend that you don't enjoy being around them when they drink, those kinds of reveals can result in hurt feelings.

But *you* aren't hurting their feelings, they are hurting their own feelings. You do not have the power to make someone happy and you don't have the power to make someone sad or angry. You can certainly say things that they *choose* to be upset about, but that's their choice. All you're doing is sharing your experience, your opinion or your story.

If they choose to be upset by your reveal, it's for one of two reasons. First, it may be because, on some level, they agree with you and they aren't willing to face it. The second reason is that your reveal triggered some old wound that was there long before you came along. Either way, you aren't the cause of their reaction. Whether they respond with anger or appreciation is totally their choice. Your responsibility is to reveal your inner truth—if you want to be close to them. What they do with it is up to them.

Question #2: *"Roy, if I commit to revealing and speaking unarguably, are you saying that all of my relationships will be wonderful, and that whatever issue I might face will always get fixed?"*

Answer: Absolutely not. For example, someone's inner truth might be, "I want a divorce," and I'm pretty sure that means the relationship is over. So, revealing and speaking unarguably does not magically fix all relationship issues, but it does create a space where clarity, understanding and authenticity can occur, and that is magical.

Question #3: *"Roy, are you saying I should reveal things like my income, sexual history or medical issues on a first date?"*

Answer: No. In fact, *hell* no. Relationships move through stages, and while those types of things need to be candidly discussed at some point, it's not appropriate to do so in the early stages of a relationship. For example, if you're on a first date, and a person asks how much money you make or how many sexual partners you've had, to honor your commitment to reveal and not conceal might mean saying something like, "I am not comfortable revealing that sort of information at this stage of our relationship." That is your inner truth.

WORKOUT!

I close this section of the book with a very straightforward question: Are you willing to reveal rather than conceal, as best you can, moment by moment?

WORKOUT #6

STRENGTHENING YOUR RELATIONSHIP TO YOUR ENERGY

BLOCKED or FLOWING

"You have a wellspring of beautiful energy inside of you. When you are open you feel it; when you are closed you don't. True spiritual teachings are about this energy and how to open to it."
~ Michael Singer

— 20 —

ENERGY

&

The Search for Aliveness

"I do not believe people are looking for the meaning of life as much as they are looking for the experience of being alive."
~ Joseph Campbell

If you pay attention to what's going on inside of you, you'll notice that deep within your heart, there's a tremendous ocean of energy. In Chinese medicine, this energy is called *Chi*, in India it's called *Shakti*, and in the West, it's called *Spirit*. No matter what word is used to describe the life-force, when your heart is open and your inner energy is flowing, you feel happy, enthusiastic, excited, passionate and joyful. In other words, you feel *alive*.

But when this energy is blocked, when your heart is closed or the energy is kinked and not able to flow freely through your body, you feel depressed, down, dark or drained. In other words, you feel *dead*.

What could be more important than understanding this inner energy? It's everything—it's the nectar of your life—because when it's all said and done, feeling alive is what we're all searching for. In fact, it's the only thing we're searching for.

As I said back in Chapter 2, we are not seeking the *objects* of our affection as much as we are seeking the *feeling of aliveness* that we believe those objects will deliver. For example, it's not a relationship, children or even a great sex life that we actually want, it's the feeling of aliveness that we think those things would bring. Do you doubt that? If so, consider that if we thought marriage, family and sex would make us unhappy and depressed, we'd all become monks or nuns.

The truth is, we're all searching for the feeling of being alive. In fact, it's the ultimate motivation behind everything we do and seek. ***It's never really about a person, a possession, a paycheck or even being popular. It's about the payoff that those things seem to promise.*** Even when we're choosing mundane things like what movie to see or what clothes or car to buy, or even what to eat, our choice is based on what we believe will make us feel most alive. Everything we do is a means to that end, and that end is to feel alive.

THE ABUNDANT LIFE

Yet, how many people do you know who feel consistently alive, enthusiastic and joyful? How many wake up every morning saying,

> "I'm back! Wow, this is great! I can't wait to see what happens today! I wonder who I'll meet or what problems I'll encounter? Maybe I'll get to experience anger or great loss, or maybe I'll even get to feel scared or terribly lonely. Who knows? But I'm so excited to see what unfolds today. I might win the lottery or need to file for bankruptcy! I don't know what's going to happen but it's going to be so awesome to find out!"

I doubt you know anyone like that. Is it crazy then to say life can and *should* be experienced that way? Perhaps. But that's how small children experience life. And if you know anything about the major world religions, they all say that life should be lived with great joy, regardless of circumstance. For example, the Bible says that life is supposed to be characterized by love, joy and peace, because the kingdom of God is within.[103] And the Buddha is usually depicted with a smile on his face because Buddhists are supposed to experience something called *Nirvana*. And the Hindu (yogic) tradition says life is supposed to be, *Sat-Chit-Ananda*—eternal-conscious-ecstasy.

"The heart is the place through which energy flows to sustain you. This energy inspires you and raises you. It is the strength that carries you through life. It is the beautiful experience of love that pours through your whole being. This is meant to be going on inside of you at all times."
~ Michael Singer

Whether it's called Heaven, Nirvana or Sat-Chit-Ananda, we're supposed to feel alive all the time. Our hearts are meant to be open to the blissful flow of *Spirit, Chi* or *Shakti*. It's our birthright to feel the life-force filling our hearts so that we feel consistently enthusiastic, motivated, passionate, excited and joyful. And if we don't, it means something is wrong.

Just as pain in the physical body means something is wrong, so a lack of aliveness in the energetic body means something is wrong.

And what's wrong is we're blocked. The energy is there and available, but it's unable to flow. And without our inner energy being allowed to flow freely through our bodies, we will always feel—to one degree or another—drained, down, depleted, discouraged, dark or depressed. In other words, *dead.*

---

[103] Galatians 5:22 and Luke 17:21

"I SEE DEAD PEOPLE"

In the movie, *The Sixth Sense*, the little kid (Haley Joel Osment) famously said, "I see dead people." What's interesting, however, is what he said right after that (I swear the kid was some kind of spiritual guru). He said, "They walk around like regular people…They don't know they're dead…I see them all the time…They're everywhere."[104]

So do you, and so do I.

Especially when we look in the mirror.

Ah, but we don't feel like we're dead, do we? Sure, we feel drained or depressed at times, perhaps more often than we'd care to admit, but we certainly don't feel lifeless or dead on the inside, right? Well, if that's true, how do you explain the things we do, including the search for a partner? If we felt truly alive, whole and complete, would we obsess over or even care about finding one? And how do you explain "adrenaline junkies," or the addiction we all have to our devices? Isn't it because there's an existential boredom or lifelessness within us that makes us crave action and constant stimulation?

And speaking of addiction—or even the casual use of any kind of substance—if we felt truly alive on the inside, would there be any need to alter our state of consciousness? Aren't all drugs either an attempt to get high or numb the feeling of not being high? Would there be any need for a mood-altering substance, anything from caffeine to cocaine, if our hearts were open and our inner energy was flowing? In other words, would we need ecstasy if we were already in ecstasy? I think the answer is obvious.

---

[104] Here's the scene: https://bit.ly/2aE8IPE

THE ENERGY CRISIS

There truly is an energy crisis, and if the relationship you have to your inner energy isn't strong, your life is literally in jeopardy. Is that too strong of a statement? Well, consider that if a person's life-force gets blocked enough, they will commit suicide. And the medical field is discovering more and more that the root cause of many illnesses, and perhaps even some forms of cancers, are the result of blocked energy. *But more germane to our discussion is the fact that blocked energy will ruin your love life.* No one is attracted to down, dark and depressed people, which is what happens when our hearts are closed and our inner energy isn't allowed to flow. To put it bluntly...

Dead people aren't desirable.

So, whether the result is suicide, sickness or merely staying single, there is an energy crisis and learning how to unblock your inner energy is an extremely important issue in life. What's strange, however, is that as important as this subject is, most of us know next to nothing about it. That's mostly because we live in the West where we're obsessed with the physical and material dimensions of life and rather disinterested in the spiritual and energetic dimensions.

For example, we know a lot about the physical heart. We know its valves have to open and close properly, and we know that the arteries have to be free of plaque so that the blood can circulate, keeping us *physically* alive. But we don't know nearly as much about the spiritual heart, and this is where the Eastern wisdom traditions make an incredibly significant contribution to humanity.

For thousands of years, the East has been learning about the spiritual heart. Practices like *Acupuncture, Reiki, Qigong, Tai Chi, Chakra work, Pranayama* (breathwork), *Tantra, Meditation, Chanting* and *Asanas* (yoga postures) are all practices and techniques that work with our inner energy. And what they've learned is that the spiritual heart is very much like the physical heart. It, too, has "valves" that open and close. It, too, has "arteries" that can become blocked and clogged with "plaque." And when that happens, the "blood"—*Chi, Shakti, Spirit*—can't circulate through the body and keep us feeling *energetically* alive.

The good news is that in order to feel truly alive—to be in "the zone," or "filled with the Spirit,"—you don't have to do all of those practices (though it wouldn't hurt). All that really matters is that you understand what blocks your inner energy and how to remove those blocks. And in the next chapter, I'll explain all of that—in a playful sort of way.

WORKOUT!

I'm giving you the day off. Take a break and rest up, because the "workout" at the end of the next chapter is one of the most grueling in the whole book.

— 21 —

ENERGY

&

How to Feel Down & Depressed

"You have a phenomenal amount of energy inside of you. The only reason you don't feel this energy all the time is because you block it. You block it by closing your heart, by closing your mind, and by pulling yourself into a restrictive space inside. This closes you off from all the energy."

~ Michael Singer

Happiness is overrated.

So is enthusiasm, passion, excitement, love and joy. It's all a crock.

I guess I should back up a bit, because that might be a bit confusing. Allow me to introduce myself. My name is *Dead Dan* and I'm one of those dead people that stupid-ass kid from *The Sixth Sense* said he saw walking around everywhere. And believe it or not, Roy has allowed me to write a chapter in his book.

Let me begin by saying I've been dead for a long time and I can tell you, based on first-hand experience, that it's far better to feel down, depressed and unable to get out of bed in the morning than it does to feel alive, enthusiastic and passionate. In my view, living a life where you often feel lethargic, unmotivated and burned out doesn't get nearly the credit it deserves. You simply haven't lived until you're frequently sick, unable to sleep and have enough pills in your medicine cabinet to open up your own pharmacy.

The day will come—and I'm going to get you there if you're not there already—where you'll need some caffeine to get you going in the morning, *Xanax* or *Prozac* to get you through the day, and if you're really lucky, a couple of drinks, tokes or pills in the evening to take the edge off and get you to sleep at night. Doesn't that sound wonderful? But wait, it gets better.

As far-fetched as it might seem, if you follow my advice and live the way I do, you can get to the point where you won't feel chemistry with others, your sex drive will vanish, and you won't be able to achieve orgasm or get an erection. *Now, that's what I'm talking about!*

YOUR DEAD COACH

Basically, if you want to feel like shit, then I'm your guy. In fact, I want to be your "dead coach." Roy, that well-meaning poor bastard, is a "life coach." He wants to help you feel alive, but as I've said, that's a crock. I want to help you feel dead. And all you have to do is block the flow of your inner energy.

If you learn to block your energy consistently, you'll be a walking cadaver in no time.

And the good news is, it's really easy to do. I mean, look around and you'll see blocked (dead) people everywhere. You'll see people feeling empty without a relationship. You'll see people significantly overweight and chronically sick. You'll see people medicating their pain. You'll see people getting massages because their bodies are locked up. You'll see people taking pills in order to get to sleep. You'll see people obsessively attending workshops and going on "medicine journeys" in search of enlightenment, and you'll see people who can't go more than five minutes without some form of digital stimulation.

They do these things because they're blocked. They wouldn't need any of that if they weren't. And since I know you want that kind of life, and not that aliveness crap Roy is peddling, I want to share with you five ways to block your inner energy (plus one bonus way!) so that you can be as miserable as everyone else is. (Can you believe Roy's letting me do this?) And I promise that my advice is guaranteed to kink your "hose," clog your "arteries" and basically render you dead on the inside—just like me.

FIVE WAYS TO BLOCK YOUR ENERGY

1. Un-Owned Responsibility[105]

The first and perhaps best way to block your inner energy is to blame other people for what's occurring or has occurred in your life. Nothing will drain your energy and depress you like seeing yourself as a victim. It truly is the secret to feeling like shit. You must *never* ask how you are responsible for what's happening in your life or what you're doing to keep an issue going or what you get out of it. The key is to…

Never allow yourself to become curious about how you're the creator of your experience. Stick to being *right* and blaming others for what's happening in your life.

For example, tell anyone who will listen about your horrible parents or your snake of an ex or your manipulative boss or your entitled kids or your ungrateful siblings. Blame everyone for your life. Do not take ownership of anything and I guarantee you'll feel down, dark and dead on the inside.

2. Un-Questioned Thoughts

A second way to fill your heart with anxiety rather than aliveness is to listen to the voice in your head and believe everything it says. The mind is

---

[105] The "Un-____" framework is based on the work of *The Hendricks Institute.*

really good at making up stories that will leave you feeling discouraged and deflated. *They aren't really into you, they just want to get into your pants...You'll never meet someone special because all the good ones are taken or gay...With all your baggage, no one is ever going to want you.* Your mind is saying shit like that all the time and if you want to feel down, discouraged and depressed, never question those kinds of thoughts. Believe them.

Oh, and take everything personally, too. Whatever happens or has happened, believe your mind when it says it *means* something about you. What happened in your childhood means you're not lovable. What your ex did *means* you aren't good enough. Being "ghosted" by someone *means* you are undesirable. Getting laid off or fired *means* you're incompetent.

Paying attention to your thoughts and not questioning any of your mind's stories and interpretations is another great way to block your inner energy. When you get really good at this, you'll feel so dead and lifeless on the inside, you might end up wondering if life is even worth living! Ah, we can only hope.

3. Un-Felt Feelings

A third way to kink your "hose" and cut off the flow of your Chi, is to not feel your feelings. When you suppress or avoid your feelings, they get stuck in you and block the flow of your life-force much like plaque blocks the flow of blood in your arteries. And when the plaque builds up enough, the heart stops beating and you flatline. Likewise, if you suppress your feelings long enough, you'll flatline emotionally. You'll become numb, like a corpse, unable to feel anything.

The benefits of this are staggering. First of all, numb people are lonely people, for who wants to hang around with a corpse? Secondly, numb people end up in very lopsided and dysfunctional relationships because they don't have access to anger, which is necessary to set healthy boundaries. And lastly, suppressing feelings shuts us down sexually. Numb women don't feel wet and wild, but dry and dull, and numb men don't feel erect and engaged, but limp and listless.

Don't let anyone tell you that you can't have this kind of life. You most certainly can! All you need to do is make sure your feelings go consistently unfelt and you'll feel as dead as a door nail.

4. Un-Finished Past

The fourth way to block your inner energy is to hold on to all your past pain. Do not make peace with what happened, instead, keep it going as best you can. Doing this doesn't just kink your "hose," it ties a knot in the damn thing!

Here's something many people don't realize: Holding on to the past makes you utterly unattractive. Resentment, hatred and bitterness darkens your feminine radiance or diminishes the power of your masculine presence. And who doesn't want that?! If the past remains unfinished in you, not only will you feel like shit, you'll also look like shit to other people.

So, be sure to never let go of the past, rather keep it alive by retelling, reminiscing, rehashing, reliving, reminding, and recalling all the bad things that have ever happened to you. Keep it going. Don't finish any of it. In fact, here's one of my favorite sayings:

As long as you keep the past alive, you will never feel alive.

5. Un-Said Truth

The fifth way to block the flow of your inner energy is to leave things unsaid. Whether you're withholding a thought, feeling or something you're imagining, or avoiding a conversation you know you need to have, or telling an outright lie, one of the most effective ways to feel down and disconnected is to conceal your inner truth.

There was a time in Roy's life when he was a "dead man walking." He was living a double life, cheating on his wife with a woman who didn't know he was married. During that period of time, not only did Roy feel uneasy and often angry, he felt a mysterious distance between himself and his seven-year-old son, and even his professional life suffered. Even though he was having great sex, he didn't feel alive.

Back then Roy was one of us. He was dead on the inside and I was so proud of him. He truly mastered the art of leaving things unsaid. Unfortunately, though, he went through some sort of spiritual resurrection and I haven't seen him since. It's a shame, too, because for a zombie, he was alright.

6. Un-Kept Agreements (BONUS!)

I would be failing in my duties as your "dead coach" if I left out the final way to block your inner energy. Roy hasn't talked about this before, so consider it a bonus insight on how to feel like shit (you're welcome).

Here's the insight: *Break your agreements.* It doesn't matter whether they're big or little agreements, just break them as often as possible. Do not be impeccable with your word. That's for people who want to feel alive. Instead, say you'll do something and then don't do it or say you won't do something and then do it. Not only will no one trust you, but you're guaranteed to feel drained, unmotivated and blah.

And if you ever feel that way, do not, under any circumstance, wonder if you've broken an agreement with someone or if there's an agreement that needs to be renegotiated in your life. It's critical that you never introspect and wonder how you might be out of integrity or incongruent in some way. That will ruin everything.

It's important that you understand that whenever you break an agreement, even the seemingly insignificant ones, it doesn't merely kink your "hose," it pokes a hole in it. Consequently, your energy isn't blocked as much as it leaks out, and over time, if you poke enough holes in your "hose," you won't have any "water pressure," at all. By breaking your agreements, your life-force will be reduced to a trickle and you'll feel blah and unmotivated all the time.

Oh, and one last thing. In order to feel drained and depleted, don't go back and make amends for any broken agreements that have occurred in the past. Just tell yourself, "That was a long time ago. It doesn't matter. I bet they've forgotten about it anyway." Don't patch up any old holes. Leave them open. That way, even if you were to make the mistake of keeping your agreements from here on out, your inner energy will always leak out through those old holes and you'll never feel really good.

LET'S HANG OUT!

Well, there you have it. If you want to feel down and depressed, if you want to feel a true lack of aliveness, vitality, enthusiasm and passion, all you need to do is block your inner energy by doing any (or better yet, all!) of the six things I just described. And when you do, look me up and we'll hang out together. Perhaps we'll see that whiny little *Sixth Sense* kid and we can both flip him the bird.

WORKOUT!

OK, that's enough of *Dead Dan.* I hope you enjoyed a little "reverse psychology" and even chuckled a few times. Now, before we move on to the next chapter, I want to give you a very challenging "workout," one that concerns only *Un-Kept Agreements* (we've already addressed the other five).

Please don't skip this. It may take weeks to complete, but if feeling alive means anything to you, it will be worth it. The "workout" has three parts:

1. Make a list of every broken agreement, big or small, with anyone you can remember. Include your parents, siblings, kids, exes, partners, people you've dated, friends, bosses, co-workers, classmates, coaches, therapists, teammates, and even casual acquaintances…everyone (if your list isn't as long as your arm, you're kidding yourself).

2. Deal with every single one of them as best you can. If that means making a call or writing an email, do it. If that means a face-to-face apology, do that. If it means making amends in some way, do it. If it means facing someone's anger, face it.

3. Make a list of all your current commitments, both personally and professionally. Include everything from your commitment to call your mother once a week, to coaching your kid's soccer team, to being in the church choir, to agreeing to get that project at work done by the end of the month. Then, for every single commitment in your life, ask yourself if you have what's called a "whole-body YES!" about it. If there's something you're doing that is sucking the life out of you, then figure out how to renegotiate that commitment. Just be sure to do it in the most graceful and responsible manner possible.

— 22 —

ENERGY

&

Expressing Your Sexual Essence

"If a man has a masculine sexual essence, then his priority is his mission, his direction toward greater release, freedom, and consciousness. If a woman has a feminine sexual essence, then her priority is the flow of love in her life, including her relationship with a man whom she can totally trust, in body, emotion, mind, and spirit. Man and woman must support each other in their priorities if the relationship is going to serve them both."
~ David Deida

Having established the importance of our inner energy and explained how to unblock it, we can now talk more specifically about what that energy looks like when it's flowing freely through the *masculine* or *feminine* form. For when that happens, intense attraction occurs and sustainable intimacy becomes possible.

When a feminine person's energy is unblocked and the *Chi, Shakti* or *Spirit* is flowing freely through her body, it appears as *Radiance*, and her deepest desire is to be *seen*. Likewise, when a masculine person is unblocked and his inner energy is flowing, it appears as *Presence*, and his deepest desire is to be *trusted*.[106]

---

[106] On a human level, not an intrinsic level, as was discussed in Chapter 16.

Therefore, a satisfying and fulfilling relationship is one in which the masculine person *sees* the feminine and the feminine person *trusts* the masculine. Learning what that means and how to do it is what this chapter is all about.

DEFINITIONS & PRINCIPLES

Before we get to that, however, I want to make a couple of preliminary comments about masculine/feminine dynamics, because this subject is wildly misunderstood.[107]

Let's begin by defining the terms "masculine" and "feminine." I hope it goes without saying that I'm not referring to the kind of macho jerks or bimbo babes you might see on a reality TV show. Masculine presence has nothing to do with the size of a man's ego, biceps or wallet, and feminine radiance has nothing to do with the size of a woman's heels, breasts or butt. When we talk about masculine and feminine, we are, in fact, talking about the two faces of God. They are the two halves of the Whole, the duality of Reality. These energies are described in many ways: *Yin* and *Yang, Shiva* and *Shakti, Spirit* and *Flesh, Matter* and *Energy, Consciousness* and *Light.* **They are divine energies expressed through human bodies.**

And while everyone has both of these energies within them, the majority of males identify more closely with the masculine, and the majority of females identify more closely with the feminine. *But not always.*[108] It's rare,

---

[107] To fully explore all the nuances of masculine/feminine dynamics would require many pages and that's unnecessary in this context. If you desire a more complete exploration of this topic, you can read my book, *Attracting Lasting Love* (esp. Barrier 6), and/or watch my two video eCourses, *The Radiant Woman* and *The Superior Man*). All of that can be found at: www.coachingwithroy.com.

[108] This is where, in this writer's opinion, Dr. Jordan B. Peterson and Dr. John Gray make a mistake. They equate the masculine with men and the feminine with women. But that is not always true. Some women are more identified with the masculine, while some men are more identified with the feminine. This misunderstanding gives rise to the gender identity controversy going on in the world today. There are people who (rightly) feel that their essence energy (masculine or feminine) doesn't match their physiology and they have a right to want that reality to be recognized and respected.

but sometimes a person's sexual essence does not coincide with their gender.[109]

GO & FLOW

That said, the masculine is a "go" energy. It's at home in thinking, planning, directing and achieving, and the feminine is a "flow" energy. It's at home in feeling, enjoying, nurturing and connecting.[110]

"The Feminine force is not goal-oriented and directional, so the Feminine heroine is not a warrior who cuts through obstacles. Rather, she is a goddess who opens doors with love. A Masculine warrior slices through impediments to freedom and truth; a Feminine goddess shines with love's radiance, opening passageways to the heart."
~ David Deida

But the fact that they are different doesn't mean that one is better or more valuable than the other. While the masculine and feminine energies are polar opposites in terms of their priorities, preferences and presentations, *they are equal in value.*

Finally, these two energies are extremely attracted to one another. Because they are two halves of the one Whole, they are magnetically drawn to each other and desire to merge. As David Deida puts it, "In intimacy, when one partner's masculine energy is brought near the other partner's feminine energy, an attractive force of sexual polarity pulls them

---

[109] If you are unsure about which energy you are most identified with, reach out to me. I have self-tests and other tools to help you get clarity on this issue. Additionally, because it is rare that a person's energy does not align with their gender, I'll refer to the masculine as "him" and the feminine as "her." If those pronouns don't match your essence, simply flip them around.
[110] This is not to say women aren't interested in achieving, it's just that when they are, they're in their masculine energy, just as a man is in his feminine energy when he's interested in connecting.

together."[111] This is true in both straight and gay relationships. **Attraction is not based upon opposite equipment, but upon opposite energy.** In other words, if two people are sexually attracted to each other, it's not because one has a penis and the other a vagina. It's because one carries masculine energy and the other feminine energy.

MUTUAL GIVING

Having laid that foundation, we're now able to talk about how to use our masculine or feminine sexual essence to create attraction and intimacy. And as I said, when a woman is unblocked, and therefore, energetically alive, she's *radiant*, and what she most wants is to be seen. And when a man truly *sees* her, she will give herself completely to him. Correspondingly, when a man is unblocked and alive, he's *present*, and what he most wants is to be *trusted*. And when she gives him that, he will devote his life completely to her. In other words,

If you learn how give the other person what they most long to receive, they'll want to be with you. It's as simple as that.

So, men, do you know how to see a woman? And ladies, do you know how to trust a man? *This is one of the most important questions in the entire book.* If you learn how to do this, your love life will be a passionate adventure. If you don't, it will be a lonely nightmare. So, I want to offer some very practical insights on *seeing* and *trusting*, and I'll address the men first.

---

[111] *The Way of the Superior Man,* by David Deida. This is, in my opinion, the best spiritual growth book ever written for masculine beings. All Deida quotes are taken from this book or its counterpart, *Dear Lover,* which is written for feminine beings. However, Deida's seminal work is *Intimate Communion.* In it, he gives a brilliant overview of masculine/feminine dynamics, and for the deepest understanding of this subject, I suggest you start there.

PRESENCE IS EXPRESSED AS ATTENTION

To truly *see* a woman means that you pay attention to her. While that sounds elementary, it's actually quite involved. Being present with a woman means that when you're with her, *you're really with her.* It means you're giving her your undistracted and undivided attention. You aren't preoccupied, distant or distracted by your own thoughts, worries or projects, nor are you up in your head trying to figure out what to say when it's your turn to talk.

Whether you're meeting her for the first time or making love to her for the thousandth time, when you're with her, you're in her world, not your own. *Being present with a woman means that she is the only thing that exists in the universe in that moment.* You're completely tuned into her, tracking with what she's saying, feeling and wanting. This is what it means to really see her, to truly *get* her.

And, oh man, can she feel it. Don't ask me how, she just can. It's some sort of superpower. She can tell if you're truly present or if you're the least bit distracted. But when you're 100% with her, when she feels your energetic presence filling her heart, she will want your physical presence to fill her body.

Let's get more specific. Here are three ways a man can pay attention to a woman.

1. Pay attention with your head. This is the easiest of the three and it means to pay attention to her words, to truly hear and understand her. The skill here is to create a space where she feels *invited* to fully express herself. This might mean putting your phone away and looking into her eyes or it might mean turning off the TV or perhaps even taking her to a private place where the two of you can really talk. By doing such things, you're saying, "I really want to hear what's going on for you." That's incredibly sexy to a woman.

When you've created a space where the two of you can connect, listen to what she's saying, and in fact, invite her to say more. Don't interrupt, judge, defend or advise. Just listen, and when she's ready for you to respond, simply repeat back to her what you think she said and ask if you're understanding her correctly. If you aren't, she'll clarify.

For example, let's say you've met a woman, perhaps for the first time, and you ask her how her day is going. She's probably not sure if you really want to know, so she might simply say, "My boss is a pain in the ass. It was a crazy day."

Pay attention. *See* her. There's way more to that story than she's letting on. Invite her to say more by saying, "I want to hear more about that, but it's noisy in here. Let's go outside so we can talk." When you get there, face her, look into her eyes and say, "So, what happened? How is your boss being a pain in the ass?"

Now, this has to be genuine. You can't fake interest just to get her to like you. She'll be able to tell (it's that superpower thing again). If she feels you're genuinely interested in knowing her, she'll trust your presence and she'll open up. She might say, "My boss got on me today for something I had no control over. I've worked there for years and I've saved his butt countless times. The whole thing is just crazy."

When it's your turn to speak, you literally repeat back to her what she just told you and ask if you understood her correctly. If you did, you can go to step two. If not, she'll clarify.

2. Pay attention with your heart. This means to understand her *feelings*. In other words, as you're listening with your head, try to feel the emotion behind her words. Is she angry, sad, scared? How does she feel about what she's saying? Is she frustrated, overwhelmed, worried? From your heart, feel into hers, and when it's your turn to speak, report from your head as to what you heard her say, but also report from your heart as to what you believe she's feeling.

Back to our example. You might say, "Wow, it sounds like you're really frustrated and maybe a little sad?" She'll respond, offering you more of her heart. And it won't matter if you've misread her feelings. She's not expecting you to be psychic. What she longs for is your genuine desire to know and *see* her.

3. Pay attention with your gut. Once you're tracking with her words and feelings, you're ready for the most difficult step of all, which is to understand what she most deeply wants. As you're hearing her words and listening for the feelings behind them, you're also tuning in to what she's wanting from the situation she's telling you about.

Here's how it might look in our example. "It sounds like you feel unappreciated and that you want your boss to know how much value you've brought to him and your position in the company, right?" And again, she'll either tell you're right or she'll clarify.

This is what it means to pay attention to a woman, and the challenge is to be present like this *whenever you are with her.* Of course you aren't able to spend every waking minute of your day with her—she wouldn't want that and neither would you—but when you are with her, *be with her.* Whether you're chatting at a party, on a date or making love, your challenge is to give her your presence by consciously paying attention to what she's saying, feeling and wanting. Doing this will brighten her radiance and she'll light up your life, giving you her heart, body and soul.

"One of the deepest feminine pleasures is when a man stands full, present, and unreactive in the midst of his woman's emotional storms. When he stays present with her, and loves her through layers of wildness and closure, then she feels his trustability, and she can relax."

~ David Deida

However, one caveat is in order before we transition to how the feminine expresses its sexual essence. Paying attention to a woman doesn't mean a man is supposed to remain physically or emotionally present if she's being mean, hyper-critical, or abusive. No one is called to be someone's emotional (or physical) punching bag.

Therefore, what a man is truly called to pay attention to is not the woman herself, but the divine Radiance shining through her. If her "emotional storm" is one where she's channeling darkness rather than radiance, a superior man "stays present with her," but only to a point. If the interaction is filled with blame and criticism, a man must set boundaries for himself and walk away until she's ready to relate in a healthy way (this goes both ways as we'll see in a minute).

RADIANCE IS EXPRESSED AS SURRENDER

If the masculine's gift to the feminine is to truly *see* her by paying attention to her Radiance, then the feminine's gift to the masculine is to truly *trust* him by surrendering to his Presence.

Now, I realize the word "surrender" is quite loaded, so let me say right at the outset, that just as a man should never pay attention to a woman who is channeling darkness, so a woman should never surrender to a man who is channeling dysfunction. *In other words, no woman in her right mind should trust a man who isn't trustable.* In order for a woman to truly relax into a man and completely give herself to him—which is her deepest desire—his life can't be a mess. She has to know that his life is governed and guided by Presence and not neurosis, neediness or narcissism. Here, again, is the key distinction:

A woman is not surrendering to a man's ego, but to the divine Presence coming through him.[112]

And if what's coming through him is weak, selfish or controlling, a woman should never open her heart and fully surrender to that. But when he is—in any given moment—animated by and aligned with Presence, when he's unblocked and "filled with the spirit," if a woman wants to experience attraction and intimacy, she must be willing to surrender to that. And since the masculine is a "go" energy, that means surrendering to his ***direction***, allowing the Presence in him to lead and guide her life.

"THAT'S WHY YOU'RE SINGLE."

Not long ago, I was referred to a woman named Melissa who wanted to explore hiring me as her relationship coach. As we were comparing our schedules, we discovered that we were both attending an event the following week and so we agreed to meet beforehand and talk.[113]

Turns out that she was quite an impressive woman. Not only was she intelligent, articulate and attractive, she was also a very successful entrepreneur and business owner. However, her love life was not going well. She said guys found her intimidating, and as a result, she was not getting past the first or second date. It seemed like the more men got to know her, the less

---

[112] You'll remember back in Chapter 16, we said that it's best to not place our trust in an imperfect, unpredictable person, but in Life itself. This is another way of saying the same thing. Trusting Life and surrendering to Presence are synonymous.
[113] "Melissa" is not her real name and while this interaction was local, the vast majority of my clients are from all over the world and our sessions take place via phone or Zoom.

interested they became. She was frustrated by that, of course, but mostly she found it confusing. She just couldn't understand the disconnect.

As we sat and talked, we discussed a number of issues that can cause such a dynamic, and after about an hour, we decided to work together. As soon as we finalized our coaching agreement, Melissa stood up and said, "Well, our event is starting soon. We need to get going. And could I have your coat? I think it might be chilly outside."

I stood up, took my jacket off, handed it to her and said, "That's why you're single."

She was stunned. "What?"

"Melissa, I decided a long time ago that when we left, I was going to offer you my coat. With the sun setting, I thought it might be cold out there and I didn't think you were dressed for it. I was actually feeling good about myself that I was noticing your needs, and I was enjoying the opportunity to take care of you. I was also paying attention to the time. I was moving our conversation along, ensuring that we'd have enough time to connect but also not be late for the event.

"This isn't a romantic date, Melissa, but as a masculine being, I love paying attention to you and the needs of the moment. I'm built for that. But when you stood up, told me it was time to go and asked for my coat, you took that away from me. You became the man in that moment, directing our relationship, and in so doing, you put me in the feminine role of responding to your direction. And I felt my energy drop. I experienced a flash of sadness and anger, something like, 'Ohhh, I wanted to offer her my coat, and damn it, I know what time it is!'

"You didn't let me be a man for you, Melissa. You didn't let me think of you and care for you. That's a huge turn off, and I guarantee that's why you're not getting past the first or second date. *Men are feeling what I just felt, that you want to be the man.*

"Granted, this take-charge persona of yours serves you well in your work life, but it's killing your love life. Because what you just said to me was, *'I don't trust you to know what I need, nor do I trust you to guide our lives in this moment. I have to do it. I have to figure out what I need, and I have to keep things on track.'*

"In other words, Melissa, you essentially told me that you're a better man than I am, that you trust your masculine more than mine. So, why would I— or any man—want to be with you? I want to give my masculine to a woman who wants to receive it. I want her to trust me, to relax fully into the depth of my presence and consciousness, and allow me to guide our lives. And until you learn how to do that, you'll never have a quality man."

"What does he find spiritually sexy in you? He is irresistibly drawn into the light of your love, showing through your entire body as radiant openness and *devotional surrender*. The openness of this love-light is what your man finds spiritually sexy."
~ David Deida

THE TWO PARTS OF A RIVER

In my book, *Attracting Lasting Love,* I compare the masculine and feminine to the two parts of a river. The masculine is like the river's banks. They contain and guide the water in a direction. The feminine is, of course, the water. You could say it "surrenders" to its container, that it takes the shape of the banks and follows its direction.

But because Melissa's feminine energy was blocked, she was not able to trust my "banks." She had never let go of the emotional residue left over from her past experiences with wimpy, directionless men, the first of which was her father. Consequently, she developed a self-sufficient persona and learned to meet her own needs and take charge of her own life. And as I said, that served her well professionally but not personally. **Contrary to what she thought, men were not intimidated by her beauty or success, they were turned off by her desire to direct the relationship.**

But if Melissa's energy had been unblocked that day, if it had been flowing freely through her feminine form, she would have surrendered to the Presence she felt in me and trusted that I would take care of everything (of course, had she been that surrendered and trusting, she wouldn't be single and would never have needed to work with me in the first place).

WILLINGNESS

Are you willing to surrender to a man of Presence and trust him to direct your life, spiritually and emotionally? And don't misunderstand me. I'm not asking if you're willing to let a guy open a door for you or buy you dinner. I'm asking if you're willing to trust his direction more than your own. Of course you will and should offer him your feedback, for feminine intuition is real and wise—and if he's coming from Presence, he will pay attention to it—but in the end, if he's grounded and guided by Presence, and therefore, trustable, are you willing to surrender and let him guide your life?

And, guys, are you willing to devote yourself to a woman like this?

"You may have noticed that your woman can get lost in her moods…It is extremely difficult for most women to get out of their mood once they are in it…Your main gift in intimacy is to guide her, moment by moment, out of her moods and into the openness of loving. And then, day by day, to guide her life into greater degrees of divine love, even beyond the relationship, so that her life becomes primarily communion, gifting, and celebration. If you cannot offer your woman such guidance, what can you offer her? Why is she with you?"

~ David Deida

FLOWERS AND BEES

By now, I'm pretty sure men are asking, where do I find a radiant woman, someone who's willing to surrender to Presence? And women are asking, where do I find a trustable man, someone who is worthy of my surrender?

That's a good question, but it's the wrong question.

Remember, Presence and Radiance are magnetically attracted to one another. They are the two halves of the Whole. All you have to do, therefore, is unblock your inner energy. If you do that, Radiance or Presence will flow through your body and you will attract your reciprocal opposite.

So, don't worry about finding a partner. Instead, deal with your inner energy, the things that are un-owned, un-questioned, un-felt, un-finished, un-said and un-kept. Just as you can see the sun's shine when there are no clouds, the strength of your Presence will be felt, or the shine of your Radiance will be seen, when you are unblocked.

Think of it this way: Does the flower worry about finding a bee, or does the bee worry about finding a flower? No. The flower just sits there, looking pretty and smelling good (i.e., being radiant), and the bees fly around and land on pretty flowers. It's what they do.

The flowers and bees need each other, and Life makes sure they meet. The same goes for you. Be Radiance or Presence, and Life will hook you up.

WORKOUT!

The following "workout" is not about seeing or surrendering, as you might expect. Those things happen naturally when we are unblocked. So, your "workout" is to answer the following questions:

1. There are six ways we block our inner energy: un-owned responsibility, un-questioned thoughts, un-felt feelings, un-finished baggage, un-said truth or un-kept agreements. Which one is affecting your love life the most? Which one is making it difficult to see or trust a partner?

2. What are you going to do about it? Will you re-read that particular section of the book? Will you take one of my *Online Relationship Bootcamps,* one that focuses on that issue? Will you explore working directly with me? What's the plan?

3. When will you take action?

"The most important thing in life is your inner energy."
~ Michael Singer

WORKOUT #7

STRENGTHENING YOUR RELATIONSHIP TO LOVE

SEEK or SOURCE

"If I had a prayer, it would be: God, spare me from the desire for love, approval or appreciation. Amen."
~ Byron Katie

— 23 —

LOVE

&

The Highway to Hell

"The purpose of a relationship is not to have another who might complete you, but to have another with whom you might share your completeness."
~ Neal Donald Walsch

Enlightenment is a term that is shrouded in misconception and stereotype. For some, it refers to a person who sits in the full Lotus position chanting "oooooommmmm" all day long. For others, it conjures up images of the Dali Lama—shaving your head, wearing weird looking robes, abstaining from sex and renouncing material possessions. But perhaps the worst misconception of all is that enlightenment is reserved for special people like Michael Singer, Byron Katie or Eckhart Tolle.

All of that is nonsense, of course. ***Enlightenment simply means to see clearly.*** It's as simple as that. Enlightenment is like being in a completely dark room, stumbling and fumbling around, and then finally finding the light switch. *Suddenly you see everything clearly.*

And that's been my goal in writing this book. I've been wanting you to see clearly about a number of issues pertaining to "life, love and the pursuit of intimacy." For example, I've been wanting you to see clearly that if you hate being single and view it as a problem that needs to be fixed, that resistance to *"what is"* creates an unattractive energy that will keep you single. The second thing I've been wanting you to see clearly is that the voice in your head should not be listened to because its "wisdom" is incomplete and based entirely on the past. Third, I've been wanting you to see clearly that by avoiding or suppressing your feelings, you disconnect yourself from your heart, others and life itself. Fourth, I've been wanting you to see clearly that by concealing your inner truth, you're actually ruining your chances of experiencing a real relationship, which is what you most deeply want. The fifth thing I've been wanting you to see clearly is that if you don't feel consistently alive, passionate and excited about life, it's because you're blocking the flow of your energy, which, in turn, darkens your feminine radiance or weakens your masculine presence.

THE THREE CORE WANTS

But there's one more thing I want you to see clearly and it's this: deep down, we all want the same things. Even though we may have different backgrounds, beliefs, races, genders, ages, nationalities, political views and sexual orientations, we all want *security, approval, and control.*[114]

But before I describe what each of them mean and how they affect our love lives, I want to make it crystal clear that there's absolutely nothing wrong or bad about these core wants. We aren't misguided, immature or unevolved for wanting them. They are universal human wants. Therefore, the point is not to grow beyond them or to transcend them. That would be impossible. Just as we will never transcend the need for food and water, so we will never transcend wanting security, approval and control.

The issue is how we go about getting them.

That's the key issue. The wants are normal and natural. The question is—and let's get personal—what strategy are you using to get security, approval or control? And make no mistake about it, your life has been, is,

---

[114] This paradigm is from Hale Dwoskin and *The Sedona Method.*

and always will be about these core wants, and you are using a strategy to get them (so am I and so is everyone).

And there are only two strategies to choose from. You are either *sourcing* these wants from within yourself, or you are *seeking* them from outside yourself.

Sourcing from within puts you in charge of your well-being and leads to a life of freedom, harmony and intimacy, while seeking these wants from outside yourself makes you dependent on others (or circumstances) for your well-being and leads to a life of fear, drama, and manipulation. In other words,

Seeking from without, rather than sourcing from within, puts your love life on the highway to hell.

YOU COMPLETE ME

In this last section of the book, we're focusing on the seventh and final "major muscle group," which is our relationship to love itself.

What do we believe about love? What is its purpose in our lives? What are we expecting an intimate relationship will do for us? Well, we already have the answer to those questions. Because we feel something is missing or lacking "in here," we go "out there" and seek an intimate relationship, believing it will provide us with the security, approval and control we so desperately want. This is the "you complete me" mindset, or what I call, "having faith in love."

And it doesn't work.

As we said in Chapter 2, "life partners make lousy life sources." No person is capable of adequately and consistently fulfilling our core wants. Yes, we can experience a wonderful and deep connection with someone and share all of life's joys and sorrows with them, but that relationship will never make us feel whole and complete on the inside, nor will it ever fulfill our core wants.

"The truth is, if you are experiencing conflict in your relationships, you are likely seeking something from your partner without being aware of it. Seeking always leads to conflict of some sort, because in the end, you are looking for something the other person cannot give you. Unconsciously giving someone the power to complete you is the beginning of all the trouble. Nobody has the power to complete you. For the power that you are really looking for—the power of completeness, communion, intimacy—does not reside in someone else. The communion you seek is communion with life itself. What you really long for is a deep intimacy with your own experience—the deepest acceptance of every thought, every sensation, every feeling. And that cannot come from outside yourself."
~ Jeff Foster

But the reality is, most of us don't believe that. We steadfastly maintain our "faith in love," but in so doing, we doom ourselves to frustrating, disappointing, drama-filled relationships. So, as unromantic as it sounds, we need to lose faith in love. Here's how I described it in Chapter 6 of my first book, *A Drink with Legs*:

> "We must lose faith in the idea that love will end our loneliness and make us feel alive. We must lose faith in the idea that a partner's love will validate our worth or repair our wounded self-esteem. We must lose faith in the idea that there's a love "out there" that will save us. As long as we have even a hint of faith in love, the very love we seek will always elude us."

SPIRITUAL AMNESIA

The "you complete me" mindset, or "having faith in love" exists because we suffer from a severe case of spiritual amnesia. It's as if life has bumped us on the head and we have forgotten who we are, that we're whole and complete, having been made in the image of God.

"You are a distinct portion of the essence of God and contain a certain part of Him in yourself. Why then are you ignorant of your noble birth? You carry a God about within you, poor wretch, and know nothing of it."
~ Epictetus [115]

But because we've lost touch with our spiritual identity, we feel empty, alone and separate, and that causes us to seek and chase and hope and pray for someone "out there" who will give us what we feel like we're missing or lacking "in here."

THE WANTS: UP CLOSE & PERSONAL

Let's take an up close and personal look at these core wants, and how seeking them from someone "out there" creates drama and frustration in our love lives.

Security—When a Gazelle is alone in the wild and disconnected from the herd, it is vulnerable to attack. Likewise, there is a subtle vulnerability in being single, a feeling of being exposed or unsafe, and this happens because we can't feel that we are "married," or in a "committed relationship," to Life itself. Therefore, we seek a partner to give us a sense of security because, like the Gazelle, there's safety in numbers.

---

[115] *Epictetus* was a first century Greek Stoic philosopher.

This is an issue I'm personally familiar with. When I was not in an intimate relationship, I felt very exposed, vulnerable and separate. I didn't have a felt sense of connection to Life, so I sought it through relationships, and that caused a *lot* of drama.

Looking back, I was a serial monogamist, suffering from what I call, *The Tarzan Syndrome.* I swung from one "vine" (relationship) to another, never letting go of one unless there was another "vine" to grab on to. For me, a relationship was a source of sanctuary, safety and security, and that put an enormous amount of pressure on the women in my life. They were being asked to give me something they didn't have to give.

How are you seeking security in your life or love life?

Approval—Seeking approval is the wanting to be liked, loved, valued, appreciated, complimented, seen or noticed. When we don't feel intrinsically approved of, when we aren't grounded in a deep sense of our own value and worth, we seek it from others in a variety of self-destructive ways.

For example, when we want to be liked or loved, we will fall prey to people-pleasing, which makes it nearly impossible to set boundaries and say "no." When we want to be appreciated or complimented, we will tend to repress our needs, over-function in relationships and potentially become doormats. When we want to be seen or noticed, we can become inauthentic, adopting whatever image is necessary in order to be recognized or considered special by others.

How are you seeking approval in your life or love life?

Control—Whenever we're triggered or upset, it's because we're experiencing some sort of perceived threat to our ego. In other words, it seems like some part of our identity is at risk or in danger. This fear makes us want to control our environment. We want to control people. We want them to be a certain way, act a certain way and do certain things. We want to control circumstances, too, whether it's our finances, our health or what people say about us. To the ego, life is a scary place and so it clamors for control.

We're all familiar with the stereotypical control-freak, the bossy, know-it-all, domineering, narcissistic type of person (hell, we probably are that person), but control also shows up in much more subtle ways. Passive-aggressiveness, peacemaking, rescuing, perfectionism, fear of commitment and criticism all stem from wanting control.

How are you seeking control in your life or love life?

THE ROOT OF ALL DRAMA

The point of what's been said so far is that not only are intimate relationships a lousy source of security, approval and control, but seeking those things from outside ourselves creates all sorts of drama, dysfunctional behaviors and painful results. Whenever we're in any type of conflict, or whenever we're triggered, frustrated, anxious, stressed or angry, it's because we're wanting security, approval or control and we're not getting it. In other words, we're never upset for the reasons we think we are. **It's never because of what someone else is or isn't doing, even though on the surface it looks that way. It's always because we're wanting them to give us something they don't have to give. This is the root of all drama.**

When you *see clearly* the truthfulness of this in your experience, as I'm sure you do, you'll begin to wonder how to source these normal and natural wants from within yourself and avoid drama. And that's what we'll turn our attention to now.

HOW TO SOURCE FROM WITHIN

The first step to sourcing from within begins by calling to mind a situation that is currently upsetting you. Perhaps it's something at work or in your personal life. Maybe it's something financial or physical. Whatever it is, call it to mind.

The second step is to identify why you're upset. In other words, which want are you seeking but not getting? Is it security, approval or control? (Sometimes it can be more than one or even all of them, but for this exercise, pick just one).

The third step is simply to welcome that want and any feelings, sensations or thoughts that arise with it. Don't beat yourself up for wanting what you want. Simply allow the want to be here, because it is. Don't wish it wasn't here, don't shame yourself for wanting it and don't try to make it go away. Just welcome it.

Fourth, check and see if that want is actually missing or lacking—*in this now moment.* Remember, when we're triggered or upset, it's because we think we're lacking one or all of the core wants. We *think* they're missing and we're looking to get what we *think* is not here. So, the fourth step is to check and see if that's actually true.

In this now moment, if you don't go into the future and if you don't go into the past, if you don't go out there to "them" or to "it," is there really anything missing? Check and see.

The practice is to experience that in this now moment, there's enough. There's enough security. There's enough approval. There's enough control. In mantra-like fashion, repeat the following sentences to yourself:

- *"I have all the security I need right now, right here. Regardless of my relationship status or the size of my bank account, I am secure— now."*
- *"I have enough love, acceptance and approval in this now moment. I am approved of and I don't need to seek it. There's enough approval—now."*

- *"I have enough control over what can be controlled, and everything that needs to be controlled, is. In this moment, when I don't go into the future or into the past, everything is unfolding perfectly, and I welcome it being just the way it is—now."*

The fifth and final step is a peculiar but powerful question:

Can you rest as that which doesn't need security, approval or control to simply be?

Can you recognize and relax into the awareness that no matter what people do, or how life unfolds, you are OK? Can you feel that nothing is missing in this now moment, and that you are complete? If you can't, repeat steps three through five until you feel the inner tension (wanting, seeking) relax.

"There is nowhere you need to go and nothing you need to do in order to be who you already are."
~ Hale Dwoskin

WORKOUT!

1. For each of the three core wants, give a specific example of how you seek that want from someone or something outside yourself.

2. Regarding those three examples, are you willing to "source from within" by following the process outlined above for each of the three?

3. Finally, Jim Dethmer has created a nine-minute guided meditation on the core wants. It's incredibly powerful and you can listen to it here: https://bit.ly/2VvrXk8.[116]

---

[116] There are many wonderful resources just like this one found at www.conscious.is.

282

— 24 —

LOVE

&

Rewriting Your Love Story

"Here's the core agreement of a conscious relationship: Let's create an environment where we are together to work on ourselves rather than working on each other."

~ Michael Singer

One of the most powerful issues to explore in your life is how your childhood and your past experiences have affected and influenced your view of love and intimacy. Given your background, what stories do you hold, what messages did you receive and what beliefs do you have about intimate relationships?

These are enormously important questions because beliefs control actions. For example, if you believed the earth was flat, you wouldn't get in a little dinghy and sail off into the sunset. Likewise, if you have some sort of negative or false belief about intimate relationships, you'll either create a destructive pattern, attract someone who will prove your story to be true, or you won't let anyone get close to you in the first place. Either way, your love life will be a nightmare.

So, to ensure that nothing stands between you and a wonderful relationship, the first part of this chapter describes five possible "love stories" that can ruin your relationship to love, and the last part of the chapter will show you how to rewrite them.

Love Story #1: Love is Heaven

This is, by far, the most common belief or story about love and intimacy, and since the last chapter addressed it directly, I'll keep my comments very brief.

The "love is heaven" story is communicated through just about every fairy tale, love song and romantic comedy ever made. Love is believed to be the pathway to happiness or paradise or wholeness. The message is that unless or until you find "the one," your soulmate, you will be "locked out of heaven," as Bruno Mars says[117], destined for a life of mediocrity instead of magnificence. But because "life partners make lousy life sources," this story always results in drama, disappointment and probably divorce.

Is this your "love story," that love is heaven?

Love Story #2: Love is Sacrifice

If a couple has been married for forty or fifty years, people always ask, *what's the secret to a long and happy marriage?* And the couple's answer is usually something about being willing to sacrifice, compromise or be unselfish. Normally we smile at such an answer, because the idea that relationships require sacrifice is believed by more than just old married couples. In fact, next to "love is heaven," this may be the most common "love story" of all. But make no mistake about it, *it is a story* (just like the earth being flat was a story) and believing it can have a devastating effect on your love life.

Back in Chapter 3, I suggested that being single is not something happening "to you" but "by you." In other words, you are keeping yourself single—*for some reason.* Well, this might be it. If you believe that "love is sacrifice," that a relationship is about compromise and giving up control over important things in your life, you might prefer to stay single.

---

[117] Here's the music video if you're not familiar: https://bit.ly/19Q8MGR

I cannot tell you how many of my clients believe that a relationship will require them to adjust their lifestyles in some negative way. They think they'll have to stop leaving dishes in the sink or be unselfish with the remote. They think they'll have to share closet space or a bathroom. They worry that they'll have to give up, or at least cut back on their hobbies, or the amount of time they spend with their friends. They fear that they'll be forced to change their spending habits or the way they raise their kids. The list could go on and on. Many people believe (falsely) that being in a relationship will require them to make sacrifices and compromises that they don't want to make.

Is this your "love story," that love is sacrifice?

Love Story #3: Love is Painful

Another very common story about intimate relationships is that they are painful. If you've been deeply hurt, or if you've witnessed someone else being devastated and torn apart by infidelity, addiction, abuse, financial deception or some other horrible experience, the resulting belief might be, *if you get close to someone, you'll get hurt. Relationships lead to pain.*

Imagine being a little girl and watching your mom suffer from depression because daddy left to be with his new girlfriend. Imagine being a little boy and watching your parents continually fight about mommy's drinking or spending. Imagine being a child who regularly witnesses verbal or emotional abuse. What affect does that have on a person's relationship to love?

I have a former client who discovered that her husband was having multiple affairs throughout their fifteen-year marriage. They've been in court and at each other's throats for over seven years now, and there's no end in sight. As a result, what stories about love and intimacy are being formed in their six children? Do you think they might be learning that love is painful? Do you think they might have trust issues later in life or become overly suspicious or put marriage on the back burner so that they can "focus on their careers?"

Is this your "love story," that love is painful?

Love Story #4: Love is Earned

Many people grow up in families where love had to be earned. Whether it was academic, artistic or athletic, they were expected to be perfect or successful, and the message they received was that their value and worth was determined by their performance.

Children raised in this type of environment confuse who they are with what they do, often growing up to become uber competitive workaholics, terrified of failure, and haunted by feelings of inadequacy.

This is my "love story." In my childhood, love and approval was tied to performance. It wasn't like there was a note on the refrigerator that said, "Roy, be the best or get out," but I definitely received more attention, affection and applause when I succeeded or won at something than I did if I was average or ordinary. The message I received was that love is earned via performance.

I can personally attest to the profound implications this has on a person's relationship to love. Because the performer is driven by feelings of inadequacy and being not good enough, they will try way too hard to impress potential partners and win their affection. Relationships will become like a competition. Rather than being real and authentic, they will become chameleons, morphing into whoever they need to be in order to win the other person's love.

Is this your "love story," that love is earned?

Love Story #5: Love is Controlling

The fear of commitment is quite common, and it usually results from witnessing an unhealthy power dynamic in your family of origin. For example, if you grew up in a home where one parent was aggressive and dominant, and the other parent was passive and submissive, you might resent the "power" parent for being selfish and controlling, but you also might resent the "passive" parent for forfeiting their autonomy and allowing themselves to be stifled and controlled. This dynamic might warp your view of marriage, creating the assumption that those are your only two choices.

The same thing can happen if you grow up in a family where one parent makes all the money and lords it over the family, or if a parent has a violent temper, an addiction or a psychological disorder. A locus of control is established in such circumstances and the whole family walks on egg shells, careful to never set them off.

If you experienced any of these types of situations, it's doubtful that you'd grow up thinking, *I can't wait to fall in love and get married!* In fact, quite the opposite. Your "love story" would be that relationships are all about power and control—who has it and who doesn't—and who wants to get involved in that? The net result is that you'd fear commitment and do everything within your power to avoid it.

Is this your "love story," that love is controlling?

HOW TO REWRITE YOUR LOVE STORY

So, what's your "love story?" Do you resonate with any of the five I've listed? The possibilities are endless. For example, if you were sexually abused, you might equate love with sex. If you witnessed or experienced physical abuse, you might believe intimacy is dangerous. If you were abandoned, you might believe love is a fantasy. If your parents got divorced and then had a bunch of short-term relationships, you might believe love is temporary or even pointless.

No matter what your "love story" is, the important thing is that you identify it and then rewrite it.

If you want your love life to have a happy ending, you have to rewrite your script.

Rewriting your "love story" is actually easier than you might think. It doesn't require willpower or commitment like quitting smoking or overcoming alcoholism does. Those things are hard to do. But this isn't. All you need to do is ask a very simple question. *Is it true?* Is your particular "love story" *actually* true? I'm not saying you didn't experience what you experienced. Of course you did. I'm asking if what you experienced is true of *all* relationships, or was it only true in your home?

And if it's not true of all relationships, aren't you free to create any type of relationship you want?

- Instead of believing "love is heaven," aren't you free to create a relationship that isn't co-dependent?
- Instead of believing "love is sacrifice," aren't you free to create a relationship that is committed to finding win/win solutions?
- Instead of believing "love is painful," aren't you free to create a relationship that is supportive and kind?
- Instead of believing "love is earned," aren't you free to create a relationship where love is given unconditionally?
- Instead of believing "love is controlling," aren't you free to create a relationship where everyone is valued equally?

In other words, once you realize the earth isn't flat, aren't you free to sail off into the sunset? Beliefs only have power if they're believed! But if they're investigated and found to be false, then don't they evaporate and simply become ridiculous stories?

So, is your "love story" *true*?

And if this question sounds familiar, it should. It's the first question in Bryon Katie's, *The Work*, which I introduced you to back in Chapter 7. **The way you rewrite your "love story" is by simply investigating the truthfulness of it.** So, let's do *The Work* together.[118] You'll recall that it consisted of four simple questions and we'll slightly adapt them for this conversation.

1. *Is your "love story" true?*
2. *Can you absolutely know that your "love story" is true?*
3. *How do you react, or what happens when you believe your "love story" is true?*
4. *Who would you be without your "love story"?*

Let's briefly walk through each question.

1. Is your "love story" true? Well, your answer is probably, *YES*. And based upon your experience, it is true. But remember, your experience is very limited and based solely upon your past. So, this is where the second question comes in handy.

2. Can you *absolutely* know that your "love story" is true? The answer to this question is, NO. Why? Because if something is absolutely true, it must be universally true for everyone all the time. Gravity is absolutely true, but does everyone believe love is painful? Does everyone

---

[118] These are the kinds of things I do with those who work with me or join one of my *Online Relationship Bootcamps*. For information, visit: www.coachingwithroy.com or email me at coachingwithroy@gmail.com.

believe love has to be earned? Does everyone believe that sacrifice is necessary to be in a relationship? (I don't.) So, by asking the second question, your "love story" will begin to unravel.

3. How do you react, or what happens when you believe that your "love story" is true? You need to answer this question yourself. I can't do this one for you. You need to take an honest look at how your "love story" has, and is, impacting your love life. My book, *A Drink with Legs*, is basically me answering this question. I graphically describe how my two primary "love stories" (love is heaven, love is earned) ruined my relationships. You don't have to write a book like I did, but you do need to answer this question in your journal.

4. Who would you be without your "love story?" In other words, what would happen if you didn't believe that your "love story" is true? Wouldn't *everything* change? If you didn't believe "love is sacrifice," wouldn't you open your heart to a relationship? If you didn't believe "love is earned," wouldn't you relax and be authentic? If you didn't believe "love is pain," wouldn't your walls crumble?

Who would you be without your story?

WORKOUT!

This "workout" is pretty obvious, isn't it? Do *The Work* on your "love story" and see how quickly your love life changes.[119]

---

[119] For more info on *The Work*, visit Byron Katie's website: https://thework.com.

— 25 —

LOVE

&

How to Love Yourself

"It doesn't interest me where or what or with whom you have studied. I want to know what sustains you, from the inside, when all else falls away. I want to know if you can be alone with yourself and if you truly like the company you keep in the empty moments."

~ Oriah Mountain Dreamer

I could make the case that this entire book has been about how to love yourself. For what could be a better expression of self-love than accepting reality, ignoring the negative voice in your head, feeling your feelings, letting go of the past, revealing your inner truth, unblocking your energy, and questioning your "love stories?" To me, that is the essence of true self-love.

But if you want more "practical" ways of loving yourself, I thought I'd finish this book by sharing some specific self-love practices from my former coach and now colleague, Diana Chapman.[120] She is an absolute genius in the art of self-love and what follows are a number of things she does to love herself.

---

[120] Aside from being my personal coach, Diana Chapman (along with Jim Dethmer) is the co-author of *The 15 Commitments of Conscious Leadership* and the co-founder of *The Conscious Leadership Group.*

SELF-LOVE PRACTICES

1. Practice being appreciated by others. Ask one person every day to share something they appreciate about you. If necessary, send emails or post on Facebook, asking people to reflect on what they most value about you. Notice any resistance you experience to being seen in this way and let it go.

2. Verbally express your appreciation of others. The act of verbally appreciating someone else touches their hearts, of course, but it deepens our self-love as well. That's because whatever you notice in someone else is also true of you. In other words, "if you spot it, you got it." Maybe what you see in another won't show up in your life in exactly the same way or to the same degree, but if you notice it in them, it's also in you. So, in addition to expressing your appreciation for others, pay very close attention to what you see in them, even if what you see is something "negative." Here's a key point:

Loving yourself means loving ALL of yourself, the "good" and the "bad."

A quick example of this from my own life. In 2018, at the U.S. Open Tennis Championship, Serena Williams had a total meltdown.[121] The umpire ruled against her and she smashed her racket, screamed at the umpire and basically acted like a spoiled, entitled, little brat.

I saw it on TV and the next day I posted on Facebook that because of Serena's tantrum, I was no longer a fan. Diana immediately chimed in and asked if my reaction indicated that I had "x-ed out" or disowned the spoiled, entitled, little brat in me.

Shit.

---

[121] If you haven't seen the meltdown, here it is: https://bit.ly/2HC6tl4

At first, I said no, because I have an ego the size of Mt. Everest. But it was true. I have acted just like Serena (and probably will again), and I can't stand that about myself. That's why Serena's behavior triggered me so much (if you spot it, you got it). So, loving myself meant admitting and *appreciating* that I have a spoiled little brat in me, and that it's OK. In other words, Diana wasn't provoking me for the hell of it. She was inviting me to love my "Serena-ness," to love everything about myself and not leave anything out.

3. Create a self-appreciation journal. Every night before you go to sleep, write three things in your journal that you appreciate about yourself. Focus especially on things that happened that day.

―――――――――

"One time, after a long-term relationship had ended, a friend challenged me and said, "Can you just spend some time alone now?" The idea of being alone terrified me. So I got a cat. This helped. I entered a long period of celibacy, therapy and learning to fall in love with myself…Finally, I wasn't waiting to be loved! I took vacations alone, bought clothes for my taste only, read books undisturbed, and turned off the phone for days at a time. Then it seemed time to be in union with myself, so I performed a metaphorical marriage, and promised to love and honor myself until the end. What this meant was that instead of waiting to be married or partnered, I decided to marry myself in a ceremony by the ocean with a private ritual to celebrate. Try this: Marry yourself."
~ Sark [122]

―――――――――

4. Ask your closest friends to act-out―in your presence―your most embarrassing and self-sabotaging personas. (A persona is a fear-based false self, the "person" you believe you have to be or a role you believe you

―――――――――

[122] *Wild Succulent Woman*, by Sark. Along with *The Wild Woman's Way*, by Michela Boehm, this book should be read by every woman.

have to play in order to succeed in love, survive a threat or satisfy a need.[123]) As strange as it sounds, we grow in self-love when our friends make fun of us *in loving ways*. It's like being "roasted," but from a place of kindness and a desire to heal. Receiving such feedback allows us to feel seen, and therefore, loved. Notice how hilarious they are being "you," but also notice the essence quality underneath the persona.

5. Do some mirror work. In your bathroom mirror, look into your eyes, relax your breath, and appreciate what you see. Take your time and "fall into" your own eyes. Truly be with and notice yourself. People look at you all the time. But have you ever looked lovingly at yourself?

6. Appreciate your "costume." This requires remembering that you are an infinite being who slipped on the costume of your identity. Take some time to really look at what you like about the current character you get to play. What do you like about the specifics of this physical costume? What superpowers do you have? What lessons do you get to learn by wearing your costume? What is the funniest or best part of wearing this costume?

7. Invite morning tears. Every morning look for something, online or otherwise, that makes you cry. It might be something beautiful or heartbreaking. The practice is to open your heart, allowing it to be touched, moved or broken. It's truly an act of self-love to keep your heart open and tender. As the tears flow, open your breath and your body, allowing every sensation to be fully experienced (there are many websites that have scores of videos to inspire your tears).

8. Create a movie poster that captures the person you want to become and the life you want to live (do not include anything about the partner you want to attract). Make it authentic by giving it a title, as well as a short description of what the hero (you) overcomes in his or her journey. Include positive reviews by critics. Hang the poster where you will see it

---

[123] For a thorough explanation of personas, see my second book, *Attracting Lasting Love,* chapters 15-18.

every day and select 3 songs that will be a part of the soundtrack and listen to them every day as you look at your poster.

WORKOUT!

Aside from doing the things listed above, I think you've done enough "workouts," don't you? Take a break. You've earned it.

"Love whatever you can from wherever you are."
~ Gay Hendricks

EPILOGUE

When Harry Met Sally, 2.0

Harry sat at an outside table at one of his favorite restaurants chuckling to himself. He was meeting Sally for the first time and he had arrived fifteen minutes early, not because he was worried about getting stuck in traffic, but mostly because he needed some time to center himself. He was nervous about meeting this woman.

They met online about a week ago and not only were her pictures gorgeous, but they had a couple of great phone conversations too. The reason he was chuckling to himself was because, instead of just sitting there and enjoying the warm sun on his face, he was listening to the voice in his head talk about Sally being "the one." *She's beautiful, easy to talk to, and from what she said on the phone, she's committed to working on herself just like you are. She's perfect for you, so don't screw it up.* He immediately noticed a knot form in the pit of his stomach. He felt scared and insecure, hoping she would like him. The whole thing just made him laugh.

After his fiancée had broken off their engagement last year, he took his friends advice and took a break from dating and worked on himself. It was the best decision he ever made. He hired a coach and their work together had truly changed his life. And yet, all those familiar feelings were still there. But that was OK. He no longer paid attention to all of that stuff.

Just then Sally walked up. She was breath-taking. "Harry?" she asked. He stood to greet her. "Sally, it's so nice to meet you." He paused for a moment and took her in. "You look amazing." "Thank you," she said. "Where would you like me to sit?" He motioned to the chair next to him and pulled it out for her.

Sitting down himself, he said, "I gotta tell you, Sally…just before you walked up, I was chuckling to myself because I'm really nervous. As I told you on the phone, I've been doing some serious work on myself, and yet there's still this scared and insecure part of me. I was thinking, 'don't screw this up,' and it sort of makes me laugh."

Sally said, "That's so funny, because on the drive over here, I felt all of my trust issues coming up. I have quite a history with men and even though we had some really nice phone conversations and you seem quite genuine, I noticed my mind telling me to be careful, that you might be a player or something. I recognize that's got nothing to do with you, and frankly, the way you looked at me a second ago…I loved that. I felt your presence and my defenses dropped away."

Harry said, "So what you're saying is that you're as neurotic as I am." They both laughed and she said, "Now that's what I call compatibility."

AN INVITATION

How to Get in the Best "Shape" of Your Life

"But prove yourselves doers of the word, not merely hearers who delude themselves."

~ James 1:22

I am truly honored that you made the commitment to read this book, but I'm afraid that merely reading words on a page (or a screen) might not be enough to get you in the best relationship "shape" of your life. Books, even one that is as good as this one is, can only do so much. In the end, true transformation takes "personal training." There's just no way around it.

I could never have gotten my "butt" in relationship "shape" by myself or by reading a book. I would have kept spinning around in circles, going from one drama-filled relationship to another, like I had for years. The truth was, I needed help. I needed the direct support and guidance (and sometimes a loving kick in the ass) from my relationship coach and you probably do, too.

So, even though you just finished this book, the reality is, your journey has just begun. The best way to truly strengthen any (or all!) of the "major muscle groups" discussed in this book is to hire me as your "personal trainer." And you have two wonderful options in that regard.

Option #1: Individual Training

Working privately with me is the best way to get in "shape," but admittedly, it is the more expensive option. However, if I took you on as a private client, I would commit to doing everything within my power to see that you understand and live the principles outlined in this book. In other words, I would get you "in shape." You can be certain of that.

To do that, we would form a very "high touch" relationship that would last anywhere from four to six months. If you want to know the particulars, email me at coachingwithroy@gmail.com and we can set up a time to talk.

Option #2: Group Training

Here is another fantastic option. I am very excited to announce that I now offer group-training programs called, *Online Relationship Bootcamps.* These are 7-week group programs that focus intensely on just one of the seven inner relationships at a time. Done via Zoom video conferencing, they are fun, life-changing—and inexpensive! You even have the option of adding private sessions—a la carte—to make the experience that much more transformative. There is a relationship bootcamp starting soon. For more information on group-training, visit www.coachingwithroy.com or email me at coachingwithroy@gmail.com.

A FINAL PLEA

Don't just close this book and put it on your shelf (or in some digital file). Please don't do that. Be a doer, not merely a reader. Take action. Take advantage of the next steps outlined above. The quality and sustainability of your love life literally depends on it. As I said way back in the Introduction:

> This book is an invitation to change your focus. As strange as it sounds, if you want to experience a great relationship, you have to stop focusing on THEM and how to find THEM, and instead focus squarely on YOU, because…

> **No intimate relationship will ever be healthier than you are."**

Let's get you "in shape"—NOW!

APPENDIX I

Additional Resources for Continued Learning & Growth

I playfully consider myself a type of "spiritual concierge," meaning, if you need something regarding spiritual, relational or emotional growth, I can hook you up. So, even though almost everything listed below has already been referred to somewhere in this book, I wanted to gather everything in one place so that you can easily find the resources you need to continue your learning and growth.

THE RELATIONSHIP FITNESS SELF-ASSESSMENT TEST
Before you utilize any of the resources below, first find out what your current relationship fitness level is. I've created a very accurate 30-question, True/False self-test to help you see if you're "ripped," "skinny fat," "overweight," "unhealthy," or "dangerously out of shape." Take the test here:

- https://coachingwithroy.com/the-relationship-fitness-self-test/

WEBSITES:
Here is a list of some of the very best personal growth and conscious living websites I know of. You would do well to bookmark them and visit them frequently.

- www.coachingwithroy.com
- www.theuntetheredsoul.com
- www.thework.com
- www.conscious.is
- www.eckharttollenow.com
- www.sedona.com
- www.kiloby.com
- www.enneagram.is

FOR THE SEVEN INNER RELATIONSHIPS:
If you want to learn more about any (or all) of the seven inner relationships discussed in this book, here is a list of resources for each of them. (Note: Most of the video and audio clips have a professional focus rather than a relational one, but the ideas being described apply to either, as you'll see.)

REALITY

Books:
- *The Untethered Soul* & *The Surrender Experiment,* by Michael Singer
- *The 15 Commitments of Conscious Leadership,* by Jim Dethmer, Diana Chapman & Kaley Klemp (esp. commitments #1 & #13)
- *The Deepest Acceptance,* by Jeff Foster

Video Clips:
- Radical responsibility: http://bit.ly/2lMVLqO (4:42)
- The hidden iceberg: http://bit.ly/2le2k9r (3:40)
- Seeing life as your ally: http://bit.ly/2l5z5TP (3:26)

Audio Recordings:
- Radical responsibility: https://bit.ly/2R0ibG8 (30:00)
- Seeing life as your ally: https://bit.ly/2KDrrif (30:00)

MIND

Books:
- *The Untethered Soul,* by Michael Singer
- *The 15 Commitments of Conscious Leadership,* by Jim Dethmer, Diana Chapman & Kaley Klemp (esp. commitment #10)
- *Loving What Is,* by Byron Katie
- *A New Earth* & *The Power of Now,* by Eckhart Tolle
- *The Four Agreements,* by Don Miquel Ruiz (esp. agreement #3)

Video Clips:
- How to discern between facts and stories: http://bit.ly/2lgWcg8 (2:08)
- Exploring the opposite of your story: http://bit.ly/2lgJfmx (3:48)

Audio Recordings:
- https://bit.ly/2WXMh2c (30:00)

FEELINGS

Books:
- *The 15 Commitments of Conscious Leadership,* by Jim Dethmer, Diana Chapman & Kaley Klemp (esp. commitment #3)
- *The Wisdom of the Enneagram,* by Riso and Hudson
- *The Four Agreements,* by Don Miquel Ruiz (esp. agreement #2)

Video Clips:
- Feeling feelings: http://bit.ly/2GuSaJl (4:28)
- Defining emotional intelligence: http://bit.ly/2lMSEzT (6:45)
- Understanding sexual feelings: http://bit.ly/1YP5tIs (4:03)
- Comedian, Louis CK,[124] on sadness: http://bit.ly/2rNQzLr (1:51)

Audio Recordings:
- https://bit.ly/2I5rNML (30:00)

THE PAST

Books:
- *The Untethered Soul,* by Michael Singer
- *A New Earth,* by Eckhart Tolle
- *The Living Inquiries,* by Scott Kiloby
- *The Four Agreements,* by Don Miquel Ruiz (esp. agreement #2)

Video Clips:
- Eckhart Tolle on loneliness: http://bit.ly/2DO9xXS (6:12)
- Indiana Jones & trust: http://bit.ly/1jbHU7u (2:09)

Audio Recordings:
- Curiosity and letting go of the past: https://bit.ly/2WQQg0A (30:00)

---

[124] Yes, I know he got caught up in the "Me Too" scandal, but if we only listened to people who have never screwed up, all we'd hear is "crickets." His perspective on feelings is spot on, and funny too.

TRUTH

Books:
- *The 15 Commitments of Conscious Leadership,* by Jim Dethmer, Diana Chapman & Kaley Klemp (esp. commitment #4)
- *Nonviolent Communication,* by Marshall Rosenberg
- *Radical Honesty,* by Brad Blanton
- *Lying,* by Sam Harris
- *The Four Agreements,* by Don Miquel Ruiz (esp. agreement #1)

Video Clips:
- Revealing vs. concealing: http://bit.ly/2nkx0FD (3:30)
- Jim Dethmer on revealing: http://bit.ly/2l5syZh (9:18)

Audio Recordings:
- https://bit.ly/2F0DjqI (30:00)

ENERGY

Books:
- *The Untethered Soul,* by Michael Singer
- *The 15 Commitments of Conscious Leadership,* by Jim Dethmer, Diana Chapman & Kaley Klemp (esp. commitment #6)
- *Intimate Communion,* by David Deida (for both masculine & feminine people)
- *The Way of the Superior Man,* by David Deida (for masculine people)
- *Dear Lover,* by David Deida (for feminine people)
- *The Wild Woman's Way,* by Michaela Boehm (for feminine people)
- *Wild Succulent Woman,* by Sark (for feminine people)
- *The Power of Full Engagement,* by Jim Loehr
- *The Four Agreements,* by Don Miquel Ruiz (esp. agreement #1)

Video Clips:
- The true meaning of integrity: http://bit.ly/2lgOQJH (7:33)
- Energy, integrity & agreements: http://bit.ly/2l5xY6e (3:37)

- How to make conscious agreements: http://bit.ly/2lgTSpA (2:52)

Audio Recordings:
- https://bit.ly/2ZiGt10 (30:00)

LOVE

Books:
- *A Drink with Legs & Attracting Lasting Love,* by Roy Biancalana
- *The Power of Now,* by Eckhart Tolle (esp. Chapter 8)
- *The 15 Commitments of Conscious Leadership*, by Jim Dethmer, Diana Chapman & Kaley Klemp (esp. commitment #11)
- *Conscious Loving & Conscious Living*, by Gay & Kathlyn Hendricks
- *Learning to Love Yourself,* by Gay Hendricks
- *The Deepest Acceptance*, by Jeff Foster (esp. Part II)
- *The Sedona Method*, by Hale Dwoskin
- *Wild Succulent Woman*, by Sark (for feminine people)

Video Clips:
- Kim Eng (Tolle's wife), on finding a partner: https://bit.ly/2BEqb6o (3:00)
- Jeff Foster on love: https://bit.ly/2ItKMjd (4:26)
- Kim Eng (Tolle's wife) on love & loneliness: https://bit.ly/31krSDX (22:51)

Audio Recordings:
- https://bit.ly/2It9f8j (30:00)

GRATITUDES & APPRECIATIONS

The impact that my wife, MaryMargaret, had on this book cannot be described. Not only did she provide invaluable feedback on the content and tone of the book, but over the nine months it took me to write it, we had numerous deep conversations about how each of us could better practice the principles that appear in the book. She truly is my partner in consciousness, and for that I could not be more grateful.

I also want to thank my son, Eric Biancalana, for his work on the manuscript. He was the first person to proofread the book, finding a ton of typos and grammar issues, and because of his degree in journalism and mass communications, he was able to teach me the proper use of the English language. So, I learned a lot from him in the process. I also want to thank Nikki Fallon and Monique DeSpain for their work on the manuscript as well.

Special thanks goes to Bob Davidson for his work on the self-assessment test, and Mike Brucher for his design of both the cover and the artwork for the book.

Finally, I want to especially thank Jim Dethmer. For nearly thirty years, he has been my friend, mentor and golfing buddy. Most of what I've learned about living and loving consciously has come from the thousands of conversations we've had with one another and from the example he's set for me in the way he's lived his own life.

I am truly blessed to have these people in my life. I love you all.

ABOUT THE AUTHOR

Roy Biancalana is a certified relationship coach, a spiritual teacher and the author three best-selling books. Though he is available to work with couples, his mission is mostly to support single people in the art of attracting and creating conscious, lasting relationships.

Besides his private work with clients, Roy's website, www.coachingwithroy.com, features information on his books, *Online Relationship Bootcamps*, video-based eCourses, as well as his one-year coach-training program.

Roy is a former PGA Tour player, the father of an amazing young man, Eric, and he lives with his wife, MaryMargaret, near Chicago, Illinois. For more information, visit his website or call him directly.

ROY BIANCALANA
www.coachingwithroy.com
coachingwithroy@gmail.com

407-687-3387

(That's his cell number. Use it.)

CPSIA information can be obtained
at www.ICGtesting.com
Printed in the USA
LVHW030906111119
636963LV00006B/2664/P

9 781733 301404